Cognitive-Emotive-Behavioural Coaching

This accessible introduction to cognitive-emotive-behavioural coaching (CEBC) emphasises the role emotions play in coaching and explores how coaches can acknowledge them in their work, as well as demonstrating how CEBC can be enriched with a flexible and pluralistic approach.

Windy Dryden explores both the range of issues that CEBC can deal with, including practical problems, emotional difficulties and self-development, and outlines the frameworks that coaches need in order to work in each type of CEBC. The book also includes a discussion of the central role of the coaching alliance and is illustrated with three case studies.

Written in Dryden's characteristically clear and straightforward style, this book will be essential reading for coaches of all backgrounds, including those in training, coaching psychologists and coach supervisors.

Windy Dryden, Ph.D., is in part-time clinical and consultative practice and is an international authority on cognitive behaviour therapy (CBT). He is Honorary Vice President of the International Society for Coaching Psychology, was granted honorary membership in the International Association of Cognitive Behavioral Coaching in 2014 and is Emeritus Professor of Psychotherapeutic Studies at Goldsmiths University of London. He has worked in the helping professions for more than 40 years and is the author or editor of over 215 books.

Cognitive-Emotive-Behavioural Coaching

A Flexible and Pluralistic Approach

Windy Dryden

Routledge
Taylor & Francis Group
LONDON AND NEW YORK

First published 2018
by Routledge
2 Park Square, Milton Park, Abingdon, Oxon OX14 4RN

and by Routledge
711 Third Avenue, New York, NY 10017

Routledge is an imprint of the Taylor & Francis Group, an informa business

© 2018 Windy Dryden

The right of Windy Dryden to be identified as author of this work has been asserted by him in accordance with sections 77 and 78 of the Copyright, Designs and Patents Act 1988.

All rights reserved. No part of this book may be reprinted or reproduced or utilised in any form or by any electronic, mechanical, or other means, now known or hereafter invented, including photocopying and recording, or in any information storage or retrieval system, without permission in writing from the publishers.

Trademark notice: Product or corporate names may be trademarks or registered trademarks, and are used only for identification and explanation without intent to infringe.

British Library Cataloguing in Publication Data
A catalogue record for this book is available from the British Library

Library of Congress Cataloging in Publication Data
A catalog record for this book has been requested

ISBN: 978-1-138-03927-8 (hbk)
ISBN: 978-1-138-03928-5 (pbk)
ISBN: 978-1-315-17598-0 (ebk)

Typeset in Times New Roman
by Out of House Publishing

Printed in the United Kingdom
by Henry Ling Limited

Contents

Preface	vii
Acknowledgement	ix
1 The nature of cognitive-emotive-behavioural coaching	1
2 The foundations of cognitive-emotive-behavioural coaching and beyond	10
3 The coaching alliance in cognitive-emotive-behavioural coaching	27
4 Greeting, assessing and contracting	46
5 A framework to guide and implement cognitive-emotive-behavioural coaching for practical problems (PPF-CEBC)	55
6 Lionel: an example of practical problem-focused cognitive-emotive-behavioural coaching (PPF-CEBC)	64
7 A framework to guide and implement cognitive-emotive-behavioural coaching for emotional problems (EPF-CEBC)	80
8 Edward: an example of emotional problem-focused cognitive-emotive-behavioural coaching (EPF-CEBC)	99
9 A framework to guide and implement cognitive-emotive-behavioural coaching for development (DF-CEBC)	110
10 Kirsten: an example of development-focused cognitive-emotive-behavioural coaching (DF-CEBC)	129

11 Identifying, understanding and dealing with obstacles in CEBC	145
12 Ending and follow-up	149
Appendix 1	151
Appendix 2	160
References	166
Index	168

Preface

This book is designed to be an introduction to the coaching approach that I am calling here cognitive-emotive-behavioural coaching (CEBC). As I explain in Chapter 1, I use this term rather than the more familiar one, cognitive-behavioural coaching (CBC), to emphasise the role of emotions in coaching and to stress that CBC does not neglect emotions.

Given that the book is an introduction, I want to be clear what it is designed to do and what it does not cover. The book has two main purposes. First, it is designed to show the range of issues that CEBC can deal with. Thus, in my view CEBC can deal with a person's practical problems where emotional issues are not a feature, but where the person is confused and tangled up and requires some clarity and a framework for problem-solving. I call this "practical problem-focused CEBC" or (PPF-CEBC) and discuss this in Chapters 5 and 6.

CEBC can also help deal with a person's emotional problems where the person's response to an adversity leads them to become stuck and to act like a car trying to get out of a snow drift, with much whirring of wheels but going nowhere. Here the coach can provide a framework to help the person deal with the adversity in more constructive cognitive-emotive-behavioural ways. The coach joins the coachee and working together the coachee becomes unstuck. I call this "emotional problem-focused CEBC" (EPF-CEBC) and discuss it in Chapters 7 and 8.

CEBC can also help people to develop themselves in several life areas. I call this development-focused CEBC (DF-CEBC) and discuss it in Chapters 9 and 10. While I will treat them separately as befits an introductory book, in coaching practice these three types of CEBC can overlap and the complete CEBC coach needs to be proficient in all three approaches.

Second, this book will outline the frameworks that coaches need in order to work in each type of CEBC. These frameworks serve to guide the coach in understanding what the coachee is talking about and to help the coach implement the type of CEBC in which the coach and coachee are engaged.

Third, while the book is predominantly focused on CEBC, it also shows how this approach to coaching can be enriched when used flexibly and pluralistically.

Fourth, and perhaps most importantly, I discuss the central role that the coaching alliance plays in CEBC in Chapter 4.

As this is an introduction, I do not discuss the use of case formulation to guide coaching. While some CEB coaches regard case formulation as the sine qua non of effective coaching practice, I do not share this view. I consider it to be a very useful, *advanced*, concept which is best used by more experienced coaches. There is no right and wrong view here with respect to case formulation, but readers need to understand that it is not featured in this introductory text.

In addition, I do *not* take a technique-heavy approach to CEBC in this book. My view is that how you help a coachee often is suggested by the work you are doing together and techniques are often co-created by the two of you as you work as equal partners in the coaching alliance rather than chosen off-the-peg, as it were. The main exception to this is that I discuss some of the technical aspects of each type of CEBC in Chapters 5, 7 and 9 respectively.

In Chapters 6, 8 and 10, I discuss three cases to illustrate each type of CEBC. The cases that I discuss in Chapters 6 and 8 are composite cases and are drawn from work with different coachees. The case that I discuss in Chapter 10 is an actual case and one that has been heavily disguised, but approved for its use in this book by the coachee herself. All identifying data have been altered.

In Chapter 11, I discuss, in a more focused way, a topic that has been mentioned at various points in the book: that coachees can be helped to identify and deal effectively with anticipated and actual obstacles to achieving their coaching objectives and goals.

Finally, in Chapter 12, I consider the ending of CEBC and its follow-up.

I hope that you find this book of value and welcome your feedback sent to me at www.windydryden.com.

Windy Dryden, March 2017
London, Eastbourne

Acknowledgement

Appendix 2 was originally published in *The Art of Inspired Living: Coach Yourself with Positive Psychology*, by Sarah Corrie (Karnac Books, 2009), and is reprinted with kind permission of Karnac Books and Sarah Corrie.

Chapter 1

The nature of cognitive-emotive-behavioural coaching

In this chapter, I am going to consider the nature of cognitive-emotive-behavioural coaching (CEBC).[1] In doing so, I will provide two definitions of CEBC since, as you will see, in my view there are two different types of CEBC. In defining CEBC, I will do so by addressing five points.

1.1. A definition of coaching needs to cover five points

1.1.1. Coaching approach

It is useful for a coaching definition to make clear what approach to coaching is being taken. Thus, I do this in both definitions.

1.1.2. Who coaching is for

Initially, when coaching was being developed and promoted, it was important for coaches to establish coaching's identity by stressing the differences between coaching and other forms of helping (in particular, counselling and psychotherapy). In general, coaching was deemed to be for people who were functioning satisfactorily in life, but who wanted to develop themselves in one or more areas of their life. In taking this line, it is clear who coaching is for prior to the commencement of coaching (i.e. those who are functioning satisfactorily in life and are seeking some kind of self-development). In my view, therefore, who coaching is for, prior to the commencement of coaching, needs to be made explicit in any definition of coaching.

1.1.3. Area of focus

It is important that a definition of coaching make clear what is the focus area of coaching and I strive to do this in my definitions.

1.1.4. The process and objectives of coaching

Coaching objectives can be seen as the outcome of coaching, while the coaching process points to *how* coaches help their coachees reach their objectives. Both of these need to be made explicit in any definition of coaching.

1.1.5. The coaching relationship

Given the importance accorded to the coaching relationship in the field of coaching (e.g. O'Broin & Palmer, 2006; 2010a), it is important that any definition makes clear what the nature of this relationship is.

1.2. What is cognitive-emotive-behavioural coaching (CEBC)?

You will notice that I have called this book "Cognitive-Emotive-Behavioural Coaching" rather than "Cognitive-Behavioural Coaching", which is what the approach is usually called. I have done this for a number of reasons. First, emotions are an integral part of coaching and thus it not did feel right to me to omit them from the book's title when I had an opportunity to give them equal billing with cognitions and behaviours. Second, when criticised by those who say that the approach neglects emotions, cognitive-behavioural coaches and therapists generally explain that CBC/CBT does, in fact, consider emotions to be a central focus for understanding and intervention. Indeed, I have given the same explanation myself in the past. However, as I have done so, a little voice inside me has said, "Well, if that is the case why don't we include emotions in the title of the approach?" This is my opportunity to do so.

1.3. Two types of cognitive-emotive-behavioural coaching

One of the problems of defining cognitive-emotive-behavioural coaching (CEBC) is that there are, in my view, two types of CEBC. The first type of CEBC is what I call development-focused cognitive-emotive-behavioural coaching (DF-CEBC). Here, the main emphasis is on helping coachees to develop themselves, but also to deal with obstacles to doing so whenever they are encountered. However, there is another type of CEBC which I call problem-focused cognitive-emotive-behavioural coaching (PF-CEBC). It is concerned with helping coachees address problems rather than strive for development. This type of coaching is sought by coachees who have one or more problems of living for which they seek help. They usually do so for one of two reasons. First, because they lack the clarity to solve the problem (which is what I call a *practical problem*). I call such coaching practical problem-focused cognitive-emotional-behavioural coaching (PPF-CEBC).

Second, because they are in some kind of emotional pain (which is what I call an *emotional problem*). I call such coaching emotional problem-focused cognitive-emotive-behavioural coaching (EPF-CEBC). Such people who seek coaching help for their emotional problems often do so because coaching is more acceptable to them as a form of help than therapy or counselling, which they consider to be more stigmatising. I will define both types of coaching in this section because I consider both types in this book. I will begin by presenting my definition of development-focused cognitive-emotive-behavioural coaching.

1.3.1. Dryden's definition of development-focused cognitive-emotive-behavioural coaching (DF-CEBC)

What follows is my definition of what I call development-focused cognitive-emotive-behavioural coaching (DF-CEBC). After presenting this definition, I will show how it addresses the five criteria that I have argued need to be covered in any definition of coaching (see Table 1.1).

Development-focused cognitive-emotive-behavioural coaching (DF-CEBC) concentrates on areas of coachee development and is flexible and pluralistic in nature. It is rooted in an open, respectful and collaborative relationship between coach and coachee. This relationship is a fusion between what coaches bring to the process and what coachees bring to the process. DF-CEBC's prime directive is to enable coachees, who are doing satisfactorily in life, to get more out of their life in a range of life areas. Coaches implement this directive by helping coachees: a) to set and achieve development-based objectives in one or more life domains, and b) to address the obstacles that are encountered as they pursue these objectives and their problematic responses to these obstacles. Coaches bring to the process both personal characteristics and professional expertise in CEBC. In utilising the latter, they will draw upon: a) a range of cognitive (including imaginal and problem-solving), behavioural and emotive techniques and strategies that stem from CEBC, and b) a range of strategies and techniques that stem from other coaching approaches. All interventions are carried out within a professional ethical context in which negotiated consent is paramount. Coachees bring to the process a range of strengths, capabilities and resources which they will be encouraged to draw upon during the process as they strive towards reaching their development-based objectives and as they deal with obstacles and with problematic responses to these obstacles along the way.

Table 1.1 Dryden's definitions of two types of cognitive-emotive-behavioural coaching

Definition	Coaching approach	Who coaching is for	Area of focus	The objectives and process of coaching*	The coaching relationship
"**Development-Focused Cognitive-Emotive-Behavioural Coaching (DF-CEBC)** concentrates on areas of coachee development and is flexible and pluralistic in nature. It is rooted in an open, respectful and collaborative relationship between coach and coachee. This relationship is a fusion between what coaches bring to the process and what coachees bring to the process. DF-CEBC's prime directive is to enable coachees, who are doing satisfactorily in life, to get more out of their life in a range of life areas. Coaches implement this directive by helping coachees a) to set and achieve development-based objectives in one or more life domains and b) to address the obstacles that are encountered as they pursue these objectives and their problematic responses to these obstacles. Coaches bring to the process both personal characteristics and professional expertise in CEBC. In utilising the latter, they will draw upon a) a range of cognitive (including imaginal and problem-solving), behavioural and emotive techniques and strategies that stem from CEBC, and b) a range of strategies and techniques that stem from other coaching approaches. All interventions are carried out within a professional ethical context in which negotiated consent is paramount. Coachees bring to the process a range of strengths, capabilities and resources which they will be encouraged to draw upon during the process as they strive towards reaching their development-based objectives and as they deal with obstacles and with problematic responses to these obstacles along the way."	• Cognitive-emotive behavioural; flexible and pluralistic.	• Those who are doing satisfactorily in life, but who wish to get more out of their life.	• Coachee development; • Obstacles that coachees encounter along the path towards their development-based objectives and their problematic responses to these obstacles.	To help coachees: a) to **set and achieve development-based objectives in one or more life domains, and b) to address obstacles that are encountered as they pursue these objectives and their problematic responses to these obstacles.** Coaches bring to this process both personal characteristics and professional expertise in CEBC. In utilising the latter, they will draw upon a) a range of cognitive (including imaginal and problem-solving), behavioural and emotive techniques and strategies that stem from CEBC, and b) a range of strategies and techniques that stem from other coaching approaches.	• It is rooted in an open, respectful and collaborative relationship between coach and coachee. • It is a fusion between what coaches bring to the process and what coachees bring to the process. • All interventions are carried out within a professional ethical context in which negotiated consent is paramount.

"**Problem-Focused Cognitive-Behavioural Coaching** (PF-CBC) concentrates on coachees' practical and emotional problems of living and is flexible and pluralistic in nature. It is rooted in an open, respectful and collaborative relationship between coach and coachee. This relationship is a fusion between what coaches bring to the process and what coachees bring to the process. PF-CEBC's prime directive is to help coachees effectively address their practical and emotional problems of living. Coaches implement this directive by helping coachees a) to set and achieve problem-based goals and b) to address the obstacles that are encountered as they pursue these goals and their problematic responses to these obstacles. Coaches bring to the process both personal characteristics and professional expertise in CBC. In utilising the latter, they will draw upon a) a range of cognitive, behavioural, imaginal and problem-solving techniques and strategies that stem from CBC, and b) a range of strategies and techniques that stem from other coaching approaches. All interventions are carried out within a professional ethical context in which negotiated consent is paramount. Coachees bring to the process a range of strengths, capabilities and resources which they will be encouraged to draw upon during the process of addressing their problems."	• Cognitive-emotive-behavioural; flexible and pluralistic.	• Those who have practical and emotional problems of living. • Practical and emotional problems of living. • Obstacles that coachees encounter along the path towards their problem-based goals and their problematic responses to these obstacles.	To help coachees: **effectively address their practical and emotional problems of living.** They do this by helping coachees a) to set and achieve problem-based goals and b) to address the obstacles that are encountered as they pursue these goals and their problematic responses to these obstacles. Coaches bring to this process both personal characteristics and professional expertise in CEBC. In utilising the latter, they will draw upon a) a range of cognitive (including imaginal and problem-solving), behavioural and emotive techniques and strategies that stem from CEBC, and b) a range of strategies and techniques that stem from other coaching approaches.	• It is rooted in an open, respectful and collaborative relationship between coach and coachee. • It is a fusion between what coaches bring to the process and what coachees bring to the process. • All interventions are carried out within a professional ethical context in which negotiated consent is paramount.

* In this column, words in italics relate to the process of coaching and words in bold relate to the outcome of coaching

1.3.1.1. Coaching approach

This definition makes clear that the approach to coaching that is being defined is cognitive-emotive-behavioural in orientation and that this approach is both flexible and pluralistic (see Chapter 2).

1.3.1.2. Who coaching is for

This definition makes clear that development-focused cognitive-emotive-behavioural coaching is for those who are doing satisfactorily in life, but who wish to get more out of their life.

1.3.1.3. Area of focus

Development-focused CEBC as defined here has two areas of focus. The primary focus is on coachee development. The secondary focus is on obstacles that coachees encounter along the path towards their development-based objectives and on any problematic responses to these objectives.

1.3.1.4. The objectives and process of DF-CEBC

1.3.1.4.1. OBJECTIVES

The objective of DF-CEBC is for coachees to a) achieve development-based objectives in one or more life domains, and b) to address the obstacles that are encountered as they pursue these objectives and their problematic responses to these obstacles.

1.3.1.4.2. PROCESS

The process of DF-CEBC is marked by coaches helping coachees a) to set and achieve development-based objectives in one or more life domains and b) to address the obstacles that are encountered as they pursue these objectives and their problematic responses to these obstacles. Coaches bring to this process both personal characteristics and professional expertise in CEBC. In utilising the latter, they will draw upon a) a range of cognitive (including imaginal and problem-solving), behavioural and emotive techniques and strategies that stem from CEBC, and b) a range of strategies and techniques that stem from other coaching approaches.

1.3.1.5. The coaching relationship

This definition of DF-CEBC addresses a number of aspects of the coaching relationship between coach and coachee: a) It is open, respectful and collaborative; b) It is a fusion between what coaches bring to the process and what coachees brings to the process; and c) All interventions are carried out within a professional ethical context in which negotiated consent is paramount.

1.3.2. Dryden's definition of problem-focused cognitive-emotive-behavioural coaching (PF-CEBC)

What follows is my definition of what I call problem-focused cognitive-emotive- behavioural coaching (PF-CEBC). After presenting this definition, I will again show how it addresses the five criteria that I have used to assess the selected definitions (see Table 1.1).

> **Problem-focused cognitive-emotive-behavioural-coaching(PF-CEBC)** concentrates on coachees' practical and emotional problems of living and is flexible and pluralistic in nature. It is rooted in an open, respectful and collaborative relationship between coach and coachee. This relationship is a fusion between what coaches bring to the process and what coachees bring to the process. PF-CEBC's prime directive is to help coachees effectively address their practical and emotional problems of living. Coaches implement this directive by helping coachees a) to set and achieve problem-based goals, and b) to address the obstacles that are encountered as they pursue these goals and their problematic responses to these obstacles. Coaches bring to the process both personal characteristics and professional expertise in CEBC. In utilising the latter, they will draw upon a) a range of cognitive, behavioural, imaginal and problem-solving techniques and strategies that stem from CEBC, and b) a range of strategies and techniques that stem from other coaching approaches. All interventions are carried out within a professional ethical context in which negotiated consent is paramount. Coachees bring to the process a range of strengths, capabilities and resources which they will be encouraged to draw upon during the process of addressing their problems.

1.3.2.1. Coaching approach

This definition again makes clear that the approach to coaching that is being defined is cognitive-emotive-behavioural in orientation and that this approach is both flexible and pluralistic (see Chapter 2).

1.3.2.2. Who coaching is for

This definition makes clear that problem-focused cognitive-emotive-behavioural coaching is for those who are seeking help for practical and emotional problems of living. The former occur when coachees lack the clarity to solve problems and the latter are emotional and behavioural problems that interfere with the person's life, but are not severe. Severe problems which tend to be chronic in nature need the expertise offered by psychotherapists and clinical psychologists.

1.3.2.3. Area of focus

Problem-focused CEBC as defined here has two areas of focus. The primary focus is on practical and emotional problems of living. The secondary focus is on obstacles that coachees encounter along the path towards their problem-based goals and on any problematic responses to these objectives.

1.3.2.4. The objectives and process of PF-CEBC

1.3.2.4.1. OBJECTIVES

The objective of PF-CEBC is for coachees to address effectively their practical and emotional problems of living.

1.3.2.4.2. PROCESS

The process of PF-CEBC is marked by coaches helping coachees a) to set and achieve problem-based goals, and b) to address the obstacles that are encountered as they pursue these goals and their problematic responses to these obstacles. Coaches bring to the process both personal characteristics and professional expertise in CEBC. In utilising the latter, they will draw upon a) a range of cognitive (including imaginal and problem-solving), behavioural and emotive techniques and strategies that stem from CEBC and b) a range of strategies and techniques that stem from other coaching approaches.

1.3.2.5. The coaching relationship

This definition of PF-CEBC addresses a number of aspects of the coaching relationship between coach and coachee that it shares with the coaching relationship in DF-CEBC: a) It is open, respectful and collaborative; b) It is a fusion between what coaches bring to the process and what coachees brings to the process; and c) All interventions are carried out within a professional ethical context in which negotiated informed consent is paramount.

Having defined the two types of cognitive-emotive-behavioural coaching to be discussed in this book, in the next chapter I will discuss the foundations of CEBC before showing, in particular, its flexible and pluralistic features.

Note

1 In this book, I will use, where appropriate, the abbreviation CEBC when referring to cognitive-emotive-behavioural coaching.

Chapter 2

The foundations of cognitive-emotive-behavioural coaching and beyond

You will have noticed that the title of this book is "Cognitive-Emotive-Behavioural Coaching: A Flexible and Pluralistic Approach". This shows that there are three elements to the approach to coaching that I am going to outline and discuss: i) cognitive-emotive-behavioural; ii) flexible; and iii) pluralistic.

In this chapter, I am going to consider all three elements. First, I am going to outline the foundations of cognitive-emotive-behavioural coaching (CEBC). Second, I will show how CEBC makes use of the concept of flexibility and is itself a flexible approach to coaching. Third, I will consider the concept of pluralism and discuss how it can inform and enrich the practice of cognitive-emotive-behavioural coaching.

2.1. The foundations of cognitive-emotive-behavioural coaching

In this section I will a) consider the terms "cognition", "behaviour" and "emotion" in relation to their importance in coaching; b) look at what "healthy" and "unhealthy" mean as applied to each of these three terms; and c) offer a CEBC-based framework for psychological health and flourishing that can be used to inform your work with your coachee.

2.1.1. Why cognitive-emotive-behavioural?

The phrase "cognitive-emotive-behavioural coaching" (CEBC) is made up of three words: "cognitive", "emotive" and "behavioural", which are linked by hyphens. Thus, "cognitive-emotive-behavioural coaching" looks closely at:

- The ways coachees *think* about a range of situations, about themselves and others and about a host of other factors that are relevant to the coaching endeavour
- The *emotions* that they would like to experience less of and those that they would want to experience more of

- How they *act* or feel like acting in the world
- The interdependent relationship among these three processes.

Having made this last point, it is useful to consider cognition, emotion and behaviour *as if* they were separate so that we can concentrate on the varieties of cognition, emotion and behaviour one at a time. However, please do not lose sight of the fact that humans respond holistically in the world and that we are thinking-feeling-behaving organisms.

2.1.2. Cognition

From a coaching perspective, cognition refers to the ways in which humans make sense of the world and the internal ways in which they strive to deal with it. The following are the major types of cognition that coachees reveal during the process of coaching that coaches need to be familiar with and adept at dealing with.

2.1.2.1. Problem-solving cognitions

There are several frameworks discussed in the literature on problem-solving. One that I favour that is particularly relevant for coaching has been devised by Stephen Palmer (2008) and is known by the acronym PRACTICE (where P = problem identification; R = realistic and relevant goals developed; A = alternative solutions generated; C = consideration of consequences; T = target most feasible solution; I = implementation of chosen solution; E = evaluation). These steps are ways of thinking about different stages of the problem-solving process. I will discuss this model in greater depth in Chapter 5, but basically it can be used both in development-focused CEBC (DF-CEBC) and in problem-focused CEBC (PF-CEBC), particularly in practical problem-focused CEBC (PPF-CEBC).

2.1.2.2. Inferences

As humans, we have a difficult time giving accurate accounts of what might be called "objective reality". An event occurs and we think that we can give an accurate account of what actually happened, but we often introduce into our accounts what are known as inferences (also known as "interpretations"). An inference is a hunch that we have about what has happened which may be accurate or inaccurate, but needs to be tested against the available data before a conclusion can be made about its accuracy. Often, we cannot know for sure if an inference we have made is correct, but we can make what might be referred to as the "best bet". This refers to what was probably true given that available data. Note the phrase "probably true". Something that is probably true may still possibly be false.

Let me give an example. Whenever I teach the concept of inferences, I ask the group to describe what I am about to do. I then walk over to a window and stand in front of it with my back to the audience and close my eyes. I then ask the group to describe what I am doing. Most say, "You are looking out of the window." I then explain that they are wrong as I have my eyes closed. Thus, an accurate description of my behaviour would have been the following: "You walked over to the window and are standing in front of it." The statement: "You are looking out of the window" goes beyond the available data and is thus an inference. It is a "best bet" inference given that the majority of people who stand in front of a window would be looking out of it, but in this particular case, the "best bet" inference would have been wrong.

Inferences occur a lot in coaching but in ways that are more personal and more meaningful than in the above example. Sometimes, a coachee makes an inference which explains why they may not select a development-based objective ("I won't succeed at it") or an inference which helps to explain why they may give up on pursuing such an objective once selected ("It is taking more time than I anticipated"). However, at other times, a coachee may make an inference that helps them to achieve their development-based coaching objective, often against the odds. A very good example of this is Douglas Bader. Bader joined the RAF in 1928 and lost both his legs in a flying accident three years later attempting some daring acrobatics. Despite being on the brink of death, he recovered, but was retired on health grounds from the RAF. However, he made the inference that if he persisted and proved that he could fly again, then he would be allowed to rejoin the RAF and take part in World War II. Most people would not have made such an inference, but Bader's helped him to fulfil his desire and he became famous for his exploits in the Battle of Britain in 1940 (Brickhill, 1954).

2.1.2.2.1. INFERENTIAL DISTORTIONS

In problem-focused cognitive-emotive-behavioural coaching (PF-CEBC) and in the "dealing with obstacles" phase of development-focused cognitive-emotive-behavioural coaching (DF-CEBC), you will often encounter coachees making clear errors in the inferences that they make about themselves, other people and aspects of the world. I present a list of such inferential (or cognitive) distortions, their healthy alternatives and examples of each in Table 2.1.

2.1.2.3. Basic attitudes

As discussed above, we make inferences about the world in which we live. However, on their own, such inferences do not fully account for how we respond to the situations we find ourselves in or to the situations that we may face in the future. For that full account, we need to add the concept of "basic attitudes" to the concept of inferences. I use the word "basic" here because attitudes are regarded as being at the core or "base" of people's emotional

Table 2.1 A list of inferential (cognitive) distortions, their realistic and balanced alternatives, descriptions and examples

Inferential distortion and its realistic and balanced alternative	Description	Example
All-or-nothing thinking	Your coachee sees things in black or white terms, without any shades of grey	• "Either I will do very well or I will fail"
Continuum thinking	Your coachee sees things along a continuum	• "If I don't do very well, I may do well or quite well"
Always thinking	Your coachee focuses on a negative event and thinks that it will always keep happening	• "Now that my boss has criticised me he will always keep on doing so"
Realistic anti-always thinking	Your coachee focuses on a negative event and thinks that while it might happen again, it is also possible that it may not. There is no evidence that it will always keep happening	• "There is no evidence that my boss will always keep criticising just because he has just done so. He may, but it is more probable that he won't"
Never thinking	Your coachee focuses on a possible positive event and thinks that it will never happen	• "My colleague has just been commended for her good work, but this will never happen to me"
Realistic anti-never thinking	Your coachee focuses on a possible positive event and acknowledges the possibility that it may happen	• "My colleague has just been commended for her good work and if I do good work, then this could happen to me"
Mental filter	Your coachee dwells on the negatives and ignores the positives	• "Even though most people seemed to like my presentation, I can only think of the one or two people who looked bored during it"
Balanced filter	Your coachee acknowledges both the positives and the negatives	• "Most people seemed to like my presentation and although one or two looked bored, I can't expect everyone to show interest"

(continued)

Table 2.1 (cont.)

Inferential distortion and its realistic and balanced alternative	Description	Example
Discounting the positives	Your coachee strips the positive out of something positive happening to them	• "While it is true that a lot of people said they liked my talk, they only said that to be kind"
Affirming the positives	Your coachee fully acknowledges the positives that happen to them and allows themself to be nourished by the experiences	• "A lot of people said they liked my talk and I am going to really process that"
Mind reading	Your coachee thinks that they know what others are thinking in the absence of evidence that this is the case	• "My boss was thinking that I am not up to the job"
Seeking clarification	Your coachee seeks clarification about what others are thinking by asking them	• "I think that my boss was thinking that I am not up to the job, but I really don't know. I will ask him"
Fortune telling	Your coachee makes predictions about the future in the absence of evidence	• "My boss will not recommend me for promotion at the next round"
Living in the present	Your coachee may make predictions but tests them against the available evidence and concentrates on what is going on now	• "I think that my boss will not recommend me for promotion, but as I don't have any evidence for that I am going to concentrate on making it very difficult for him not to recommend me"
Magnification	Your coachee blows things out of proportion with respect to bad things happening to them and their negative qualities	• "If I don't give a good presentation then I will be stuck at this level for years"
Keeping things in proportion	Your coachee keeps the bad things that happen to them and their negative qualities in reasonable proportion	• "If I don't give a good presentation, I can learn to improve and still raise my work level in the future if I do"

Table 2.1 (cont.)

Inferential distortion and its realistic and balanced alternative	Description	Example
Minimisation	Your coachee minimises the importance of good things in their life or their positive qualities	• "If I passed, then anyone can do so. It's no big deal"
Appreciating the importance of the positive	Your coachee acknowledges the importance of good things in their life or their positive qualities	• "If I passed then that is an achievement regardless of what anyone else did"
Emotional reasoning	Your coachee assumes that their feelings reflect reality	• "I feel anxious so something bad is about to happen to me"
Checking one's emotional intuition	Your coachee does not automatically assume that their feelings reflect reality. They check them against the available evidence	• "I feel anxious, but that does not mean that something bad is about to happen to me. It means that I think that it is"
Cognitive reasoning	Your coachee assumes that their thoughts reflect reality	• "I think that my colleague doesn't want to work with me so it is true that he doesn't"
Checking one's thinking	Your coachee does not automatically assume that their thoughts reflect reality. They check them against the available evidence	• "I think that my colleague doesn't want to work with me, but I need to check this out"
Labelling	Your coachee focuses on their behaviour and that of others and labels the person with that behaviour	• "My colleague betrayed my trust and thus she is an untrustworthy person"
Aspect focus without labelling	Your coachee focuses on their behaviour and that of others, but refrains from labelling the person with that behaviour	• "My colleague betrayed my trust, but it does not make her an untrustworthy person. I may be able to trust her in the future over certain things, but not over others"

(continued)

16 The foundations of CEBC and beyond

Table 2.1 (cont.)

Inferential distortion and its realistic and balanced alternative	Description	Example
Personalisation	Your coachee assumes that an event must relate to them	• "My team were not successful with the bid, which proves it was my fault"
Realistic attributions	Your coachee does not automatically assume that an event must relate to them. They are open to the possibility that it may or may not do so and will test these assumptions against the available evidence	• "My team were not successful with the bid to which we may all have contributed some responsibility. I need to assess this in an open way with my team"

and behavioural responses to events.[1] When we hold an attitude towards something, we adopt an evaluative stance towards that thing. Such attitudes can be flexible and non-extreme or rigid and extreme. When your coachees hold flexible and non-extreme attitudes then these help them to make progress towards their development-based objectives, and help them deal productively with any obstacles they encounter along the way. On the other hand, when they hold rigid and extreme attitudes then these explain why they will find it difficult to set and work towards development-based objectives and why they will not deal productively with the above-mentioned obstacles. Table 2.2 lists the two sets of attitudes, and describes and exemplifies them. These rigid and extreme attitudes are often at the core of the emotional problems that coachees seek help for in EPF-CEBC.

2.1.2.3.1. ATTITUDES: SPECIFIC AND GENERAL

The two sets of attitudes that I have presented in Table 2.2 can be specific or general. The examples of those attitudes that I provided in the table are specific in nature. Specific attitudes are characterised by their referents to the specific context to which the person is reacting. In Table 2.2 this is the specific job that the person has applied for and the possibility that they may not be successful with their application for that specific job. General attitudes, on the other hand, are characterised by their referents to more broad contexts and vary according to their generality. For example:

- Specific rigid attitude: "I really want to get the job that I have just applied for and therefore I have to get it." As you can see, this is the specific rigid attitude listed in Table 2.2. It is held about the specific job for which the person has applied.

Table 2.2 Flexible and non-extreme basic attitudes and rigid and extreme basic attitudes

Basic attitude	Description	Example
Flexible attitude	Your coachee asserts what they want, but does not demand that they must get their preference met	• "I really want to get the job that I have just applied for, but that does not mean that I have to get it"
Non-awfulising attitude	Your coachee acknowledges that it would be bad not to get their preference met, but that it would not be awful	• "It would be bad not to get the job, but it would not be the end of the world"
Discomfort tolerance attitude	Your coachee acknowledges that while it would be a struggle to put up with not getting their preference met, i) they can tolerate this situation, ii) it is worth tolerating, iii) they are prepared to tolerate it, and iv) they are going to tolerate it	• "It would be a struggle for me to put up with not getting the job, but I can do so and it's in my interests to do so because it will help me to apply for other jobs. I am prepared to put up with being rejected and I am going to do so, by finding out what I could have done to have been successful and resolve to do this next time"
Acceptance attitude	Your coachee acknowledges that i) they, ii) another person, or iii) an aspect of life may be bad in some important respect. However, this does not change the fact that i) they are a fallible human being capable of good, bad and neutral behaviour, ii) the other person is a fallible human being capable of good, bad and neutral behaviour, and iii) life is a complex mixture of good, bad and neutral aspects	• "If I fail to get the job I applied for, I will seek feedback and if it transpires that I did something wrong, I will accept myself as a fallible human being who did the wrong thing and resolve to learn from the experience"

(continued)

18 The foundations of CEBC and beyond

Table 2.2 (cont.)

Basic attitude	Description	Example
Rigid attitude	Your coachee not only asserts what they want, but also demands that they must get their preference met	• "I really want to get the job that I have just applied for and therefore I have to get it"
Awfulising attitude	Your coachee acknowledges that not only would it be bad not to get their preference met, it would also be awful	• "It would be bad not to get the job and therefore it would be the end of the world if I did not get it"
Discomfort intolerance attitude	Your coachee acknowledges that it would not just be a struggle putting up with not getting their preference met, it would be intolerable	• "It would not just be a struggle for me to put up with not getting the job, I could not tolerate it"
Depreciation attitude	Your coachee acknowledges that if i) they, ii) another person or iii) an aspect of life is bad in some important respect, it follows that i) they are bad, ii) the other person is bad or iii) life is bad	• "If I fail to get the job I applied for, I will seek feedback and if it transpires that I did something wrong it proves that I am worthless"

- Moderately general rigid attitude: "Whenever I apply for jobs that I really want to get, then I must get them." This rigid attitude is held about a general class of events that refer to "jobs that I have applied for and really want to get". Thus, this attitude is more general than the specific attitude listed above. However, it is less general than the attitude discussed below.
- Highly general rigid attitude: "Whenever I really want something, then I must get it." This rigid attitude is held about a much more general class of events than "jobs that I have applied for and really want", as they refer to "anything that I really want". It is, thus, a highly general attitude.

2.1.2.3.2. CORE ATTITUDES

Core attitudes are general attitudes that, when rigid and extreme, tend to account for your coachee's difficulty in recurring situations with an identifying theme (e.g. failure, rejection and unfairness). They may also explain why your coachee avoids certain situations when they think that they might encounter situations based on these themes. If you have time to work with your coachees on their rigid and extreme attitudes, this will be immensely helpful for them in the dealing with the obstacles phase of development-focused cognitive-emotive-behavioural coaching (DF-CEBC) and particularly in emotional problem-focused cognitive-emotive-behavioural coaching (EPF-CEBC).

In working with attitudes in coaching, your goal, as I will discuss in Chapters 7 and 8, is to help your coachees to identify their rigid and extreme attitudes – whether specific or general (i.e. core) – and to examine them so that they can hold flexible and non-extreme attitudes whenever possible. When CEBC is particularly successful, coachees develop and implement a set of healthy core flexible and non-extreme attitudes whereby they are equipped to deal with a range of adversities as they pursue their development-based objectives and in life in general. These healthy core attitudes are particularly useful in helping coaches maintain over time the developmentally based gains they have derived from CEBC.

2.1.2.4. Images

While cognitions are most often expressed in words, we also have and are affected by images, mental pictures that may help us to envision and pursue what is important to us or hinder us from doing these things. For some of your coachees, unless they can picture themselves doing something then they would struggle to do it. My experience is that coaches who have a rich imagery life themselves tend to focus more on this imagery modality with their coachees than coaches who don't.

2.1.3. Emotion

I mentioned earlier in this chapter that what has been traditionally known as cognitive-behavioural coaching has wrongly been characterised as neglecting emotions in coaching. This is not the case, and to make this clear I refer to the approach as cognitive-emotive-behavioural coaching (CEBC). In this section, I will discuss how you can work with emotions in both problem-focused CEBC and development-focused CEBC.

2.1.3.1. Emotion in emotional problem-focused cognitive-emotive-behavioural coaching (EPF-CEBC)

In emotional problem-focused CEBC, coachees seek help often because they are in emotional pain and it is important that coaches need to acknowledge their feelings and have a model to work with them.

2.1.3.1.1. CHANGE THE WAY FEEL YOU BY CHANGING THE WAY YOU THINK AND ACT

The most traditional approach to helping coachees deal with their emotional pain in EPF-CEBC is to encourage them to change the distorted cognitions and dysfunctional behaviours that are related to their emotional pain. The model that I use for this purpose is derived from a specific approach within CEBC known as Rational Emotive Behavioural Coaching. It involves helping coachees do the following:

- To understand the emotional problem using the ABC framework employed in REBC where A = <u>A</u>dversity; B = <u>B</u>asic attitude (rigid and/or extreme); C = emotional and behavioural <u>C</u>onsequences of B
- To set an emotional and behavioural goal in the face of the adversity at A
- To see that the best way to achieve this emotional goal is to change their basic attitude from rigid and extreme to flexible and non-extreme, and
- To act in ways that are consistent with this attitude change.

2.1.3.1.2. ACCEPT THE WAY YOU THINK AND FEEL AND TAKE VALUE-BASED ACTION

An alternative approach to emotional pain is based on a different model, as exemplified by an approach to CEBC known as Acceptance and Commitment Coaching (Blonna, 2010). In this approach, coachees are encouraged to view the emotional pain that they are experiencing, and for which they are seeking help, and the distorted cognitions that often accompany this pain as suffering that is part and parcel of living, and to consider that it is their attempts to deal with these thoughts and feelings that are the problem, not the existence of the thoughts and feelings themselves. In this approach to EPF-CEBC you would encourage your coachees to acknowledge the existence of their feelings and related thoughts and to accept them with mindfulness as a prelude to encouraging them to act in ways that are consistent with their values.

2.1.3.2. Emotion in development-focused cognitive-emotive-behavioural coaching (DF-CEBC)

When your coachee encounters an obstacle during the pursuit of their development-based objectives and they don't deal well with these obstacles then they usually experience problematic feelings about the adversity that constitutes the obstacle. You can help your coachee deal with their feelings by using either of the above two strategies.

When your coachee is working towards their development-based objectives and things are going well, then their feelings are usually positive and these can be acknowledged but do not need to be explored.

2.1.4. Behaviour

Behaviour plays a very important part in both PF-CEBC and DF-CEBC, which I will now discuss.

2.1.4.1. Behaviour in problem-focused cognitive-emotive-behavioural coaching (PF-CEBC)

When your coachee is seeking your help for a problem in living it is important that you understand the role that their behaviour plays in the maintenance of their problem. In practical problem-focused CEBC (PPF-CEBC), it often happens that your coachee is taking action that is impulsive and what they need to do is to refrain from acting impulsively and to stand back, focus on the problem(s) that they are encountering and use problem-solving methods to solve the problem. In emotional problem-focused CEBC (EPF-CEBC), quite often the purpose of such behaviour is to help your coachee to rid themselves of painful feelings or to avoid the adversity or both. While this is your coachee's intention, the effect of such behaviour is that it unwittingly maintains the problem. Such problem-maintaining behaviour can be quite subtle so that you need to be comprehensive in your assessment of this behaviour.

2.1.4.1.1. OVERT BEHAVIOUR AND ACTION TENDENCIES

When it comes to helping your coachee address their nominated problem in living, it is important that you help them to understand the difference between an action tendency and overt behaviour. An action tendency is an urge to act which your coachee has not yet converted into action. When they do, it becomes overt behaviour. It is important that you help your client to learn to identify their problem-related action tendencies and to develop the attitude that they do not have to act on their urges and that instead they can use these urges either to address the thoughts that underpin these urges or to act in value-consistent ways or both.

2.1.4.2. Behaviour in development-focused cognitive-emotive-behavioural coaching (DF-CEBC)

The points that I made about behaviour in PF-CEBC also apply when you as coach are called upon to help your coachee address the difficulties that they experience when encountering obstacles to pursuing their development-based objectives. However, when such obstacles are not encountered and your coachee is engaged in pursuing these objectives, then, when focusing on behaviour, you and your coachee need to consider the following:

- Before taking behavioural steps to achieve their development-based objectives it is important that your coachee makes an action plan detailing what they are going to do and when they are going to do it. As we will see in Chapters 5 and 6, it is important for your coachee to devise an action plan that can be integrated into the rest of their life. Otherwise, they will struggle to implement it over time.
- Some coachees consider that once they have devised an action plan, then they can rest on their laurels and that, in some magical way, that is all they need to do to achieve their development-based objectives. It is important that your coachee really understands that unless they put their action plans into practice and do so consistently over time, then they will not realise their development-based objectives.

- You need to discover whether your coachee has in their repertoire the behaviour that they need to implement their action plans and achieve their development-based objectives. If not, you can help them to acquire this behaviour yourself or help the person to source someone who can.
- You need to determine how skilful your coachee is at the behaviour that they do have in their repertoire which they need to enact to achieve their development-based objectives. If they need to become more skilful, you can help them do this yourself or again help them source someone who can.
- You need to help your coachee to monitor the effects of their behaviour so that they can learn from implementing their action plan and make any necessary modifications both to the action plan itself and to the behaviour they have chosen to enact to implement the plan.

2.1.5. The interdependence of cognition, emotion and behaviour

When I studied psychology a half a century ago, standard textbooks would have a separate chapter on subjects such as "cognition", "emotion" and "behaviour". In reality, however, these psychological processes do not occur in isolation from one another. Rather, as noted earlier, they are integrally related. Thus, when your coachee thinks about taking action in the service of one of their development-based objectives, they will tend to have a feeling about doing so and be inclined to take action on the task or inclined to avoid doing so.

Thus, when you are working with a coachee, whether it is on one of their problems of living (practical or emotional), on one of their development-based objectives or on their problematic response to one of the obstacles they may experience on the road to achieving such an objective, it is important that you keep in mind the cognitive, emotive and behavioural components of their response and how these are linked together.

2.2. Flexibility and cognitive-emotive-behavioural coaching

In my opinion one of the hallmarks of an effective CEB coach is flexibility. Flexibility is best understood when we consider at the same time its antonym – rigidity. When we take a rigid approach to phenomena we have a fixed view about how these phenomena absolutely should or must be. If they are not as they must be we may take action to try to force these phenomena to fit into the fixed categories that we have established in our minds.

2.2.1. The story of Procrustes

Let me give you an example. Procrustes, a figure from Greek mythology, was a host who kept a house by the side of the road and offered hospitality to passing strangers who were invited to dine with him and to sleep the night.

Procrustes (whose name means "he who stretches") had a "one-size fits all" bed and was rigid in the sense that he believed that everybody had to fit into his bed. So, he stretched the legs of the guests who were too short for the bed and cut off the legs of those who were too tall for it. And all because Procrustes was rigid about having his guests fit into his bed. Have you heard of the phrase "trying to fit something into a Procrustean bed"? If so, this is where the phrase comes from. As you might expect, Procrustes came to a sticky end when Theseus apparently turned the tables on him, fatally adjusting him to his own bed.

Now, what would have happened if Procrustes was flexible in his approach to having his guests fit into his bed? First, he would have allowed them to sleep in his bed without attempting to adjust them in any way. If he was keen to only have people sleep in his bed who exactly fitted it, then he would have restricted his invitations to people who matched the bed's dimensions. In addition, he might have ordered a few different-sized beds, so ensuring that his guests would have been comfortable. My hunch is that if he had done that, then Theseus would have had no reason to kill him.

The real story of Procrustes and my proposed alternative shows clearly the consequences of rigidity and flexibility. Procrustes' rigid stance led to the demise of his guests and eventually his own demise. It prevented him from thinking creatively to solve the problems and basically led to "black and white thinking": either you fit my bed or I will make you fit my bed. On the other hand, if Procrustes had adopted a flexible stance, he would have lived, his guests would have lived and he would have been freed to think laterally to deal with the problem. His flexible position would have led to "grey" thinking rather than "black and white" thinking: if you don't fit my bed then there are a variety of positions available to us to address the problem.

2.2.2. Flexibility in the practice of coaching

If you consider the field of coaching, you will soon discover that there is a myriad of different approaches. There are specific approaches within the various traditions (e.g. psychodynamic, humanistic, cognitive-behavioural, transpersonal and systemic) and broader approaches which seek to combine or integrate these different specific approaches. This latter way of working is known as eclecticism or integration in coaching.

The concepts of rigidity and flexibility are relevant to the above areas. For example, it is possible to practise a specific approach to coaching in either a flexible or rigid way, and my hypothesis is that experienced practitioners within specific coaching approaches are more flexible in their use of these approaches than novice coaches who are more likely to practise their particular approach by the book.

Coaches who regard themselves as advocates of eclecticism or integration in coaching tend to see themselves as practising coaching in a flexible manner and to the extent that they display no allegiance to any specific approach to coaching this is probably the case. However, when one takes a closer look at their practice, it becomes apparent that they favour specific approaches over others. If they exclude or downplay specific approaches then one might ask why they do so. For example, training programmes which purport to school trainees in integrative approaches to coaching tend either to exclude cognitive-behavioural elements or downplay them. This is strange since CBC has perhaps the best evidence base among the different specific approaches within coaching. Is this a sign of rigidity? It is difficult to say, but to exclude or underplay an approach which has a good evidence may suggest this.

2.2.3. What does it mean to practise an approach rigidly and flexibly?

Every approach to coaching has practical procedural rules. Thus, in problem-focused CEBC there is a treatment sequence which suggests for coaches a particular order in which interventions are to be made. When these rules are used rigidly, a CEBC coach would only use the recommended sequence even when there was evidence that this sequence was not working.

So, rigidity in CEBC occurs when coaches stick dogmatically to procedural rules and exclude specific interventions which may be helpful even if they are not generally recommended by the approach. But what are markers of flexibility? Let me be clear that I do not equate flexibility in the practice of CEBC with being laissez-faire in an anything goes sense. Nor do I mean that all alternative approaches are given equal weight. A coach who favours particular ways of working, especially when there is evidence in favour of these ways, is acting ethically when they explain this point to their coachees. However, coaches can also demonstrate flexibility when they include unfavoured methods in their coaching practice. Thus, coaches who have preferred ways of working (like CEBC), but are prepared to make compromises with their preferences, are being flexible. This is why I have indicated that flexibility is one of two concepts that informs CEBC as I describe it is this book. The other concept is pluralism.

2.3. Pluralism and cognitive-emotive-behavioural coaching

Pluralism can be defined as the philosophical belief that "any substantial question admits of a variety of plausible but mutually conflicting responses" (Rescher, 1993: 79). More than that, it is an ethical commitment to valuing diversity; and a wariness towards monolithic, all-consuming "truths", because of the way that they can suppress individuality and difference through non-deviation from a singular Truth. In respect to coaching, this pluralistic standpoint implies that there are a variety of views that can be taken on a wide range of coaching issues, and that there is no inherent right or wrong way, but obviously some ways will eventually prove to be more helpful than others in solving problems and realising goals. However, just because there is no inherent right or wrong way, this does not mean that unrestrained relativism is being advocated. Responsible or restrained relativism does not shy away when necessary from saying things are right or wrong, true or false, in a strong probabilistic manner. So the focus in coaching is on the possible usefulness of what is being proposed from whatever source at any given time. This is not inconsistent with the idea that the coach can have a preferred approach to coaching, but it points out that the pluralistic CEB coach looks outside of CEBC to help coachees whenever necessary. In what follows, I will discuss the two pillars of pluralism and a number of pluralistic principles that are based on these two pillars (Cooper & Dryden, 2016).

2.3.1. The two pillars of pluralism

There are two pillars that underpin a pluralistic approach to coaching: i) pluralism across coaching orientations, and ii) pluralism across perspectives.

2.3.1.1. Pillar 1: Pluralism across coaching orientations

This means that a coach who values pluralism is open to considering a variety of different ways in which coachees can be helped to a) set objectives; b) work towards achieving these objectives; c) deal with obstacles to the pursuit of these objectives; and d) deal with common problems that coachees bring to coaching. Taking this open-minded stance poses a direct challenge to the narrowing effects of schoolism whereby the coach stays within the confines of a particular theory or set of techniques. The practice of schoolism has been endemic in the field of counselling and psychotherapy and this can also be seen in the field of coaching. Thus, while it is possible for some CEB coaches to stay within the confines of CEBC, this book is for coaches who wish to adopt a pluralistic approach across coaching orientations.

2.3.1.2. Pillar 2: Pluralism across perspectives

A pluralistic coaching approach advocates that *both* participants in the coaching relationship – coachees as well as coaches – have much to offer when it comes to making decisions concerning coaching objectives and the selection of coaching tasks and methods. This means that a pluralistic approach emphasises shared decision-making and feedback between coachees and coaches. It draws upon the perspectives of both participants.

2.3.2. The principles of pluralism

These two pillars of the pluralistic approach to coaching can be summarised in the following principles:

- There is no one absolute right way of conceptualising coachees' issues and objectives – different viewpoints are useful for different coachees at different points in time.
- There is no one absolute right way of practising coaching – different coachees need different things at different points in time and therefore coachees need to have a broad coaching practice repertoire.
- Disputes and disagreements in the coaching field may, in part, be able to be resolved by taking a "both/and" perspective, rather than an "either/or" one.
- It is important that coaches respect each other's work and recognise the value that it can have. In this book, I hope to demonstrate this respect when discussing the contributions from other approaches to CEBC.
- Coaches should ideally acknowledge and celebrate coachees' diversity and uniqueness.
- Coachees should ideally be involved fully at every stage of the coaching process.
- Coachees should ideally be understood in terms of their strengths and resources as well as their areas of struggle.
- Coaches should ideally have an openness to multiple sources of knowledge on how to practise coaching: including research, personal experience and theory.
- It is important that coaches take a critical perspective on their own theory and practice: being willing to look at their own investment in a particular position and having the ability to stand back from it.

In this chapter, I have outlined the foundations of cognitive-emotive-behavioural coaching and discussed the concepts of flexibility and pluralism. Having made the case for a flexible and pluralistic approach to CEBC, in the next chapter I will consider what has come to be known as the coaching alliance and discuss how it informs the practice of CEBC.

Note

1 I will use the terms "attitude" and "basic attitude" interchangeably in this book.

Chapter 3

The coaching alliance in cognitive-emotive-behavioural coaching

One of the most important frameworks that informs the practice of coaching was introduced by Ed Bordin (1979), who referred to this framework as the working alliance. Bordin argued that the working alliance is comprised of three domains: bonds, goals and tasks. Later, I added a fourth domain which I called "views" (Dryden, 2006, 2011). Hereafter, I will refer to this framework as the coaching alliance. It is my judgement, and one that is broadly held in the field, that the effectiveness of coaching, no matter what approach is taken by the coach, depends on a good coaching alliance between you and your coachee. In this chapter, I will consider the issues that arise when coaching is considered from the perspective of the alliance and what makes for a good coaching alliance. In my opinion, you should be mindful of these issues when a person seeks coaching help from you.

O'Broin & Palmer (2010a: 4) used the term "coaching alliance" and said that "the coaching alliance reflects the quality of the coachee's and coach's engagement in collaborative, purposive work within the coaching relationship, and is jointly negotiated, and renegotiated throughout the coaching process over time". O'Broin & Palmer's (2010a) definition nicely dovetails with Bordin's ideas. They refer a) to "purposive work", which is equivalent to "tasks" and "goals", and b) to the type of relationship marked by collaboration and negotiation, which is equivalent to "bonds". However, they make no mention of "views".

Let me now discuss each of the four domains of the alliance in turn.

3.1. Bonds in cognitive-emotive-behavioural coaching

Bonds refer to the interpersonal connectedness between the you and your coachee. Here, several issues come to the fore.

- The core conditions in CEBC
- The reflection process in CEBC
- Your interactive style as a CEB coach and
- The bonds of influence in CEBC.

3.1.1. The core conditions in CEBC

Carl Rogers (1957) argued that there were six conditions that were necessary and sufficient for personal change to occur. Over the years, three of these conditions (empathy, unconditional positive regard[1] and genuineness) have been regarded as core and have been thus called "the core conditions". What is important for coaches to recognise is that coachees need to *experience* the presence of these conditions for them to have the potency for change.

Different coaches have different views on the necessity and sufficiency of these conditions. In cognitive-emotive-behavioural coaching, the predominant view is that it is important, but not necessary, for coachees to experience their coaches as empathic, accepting[2] and genuine. For some coachees, one "core condition" may be more helpful to them than another condition. Thus, one coachee may value your honesty more than your acceptance of them. This raises the question concerning how you can tell which condition your coachee values more than others. This question naturally leads us to a discussion of what I call the "reflection process", which is a key aspect of what O'Broin & Palmer (2010a) refer to as a relationship based on collaboration and negotiation.

3.1.2. The reflection process in CEBC

As the psychologist George Kelly[3] advised: "If you want to know what is right and wrong for your coachee, ask them, they may tell you" (Bannister & Fransella, 1986). The reflection process is interactive and not only incorporates the coachee's view, but also the coach's. This process is an integral part of CEBC, showing the state of the relationship with respect to the degree of mutual respect, acceptance and trust present in that relationship.

3.1.3. Interactive style in CEBC

The third area relevant to the CEBC bond concerns the interactive style adopted by you and your coachee and the goodness of "fit" between these respective styles. In CEBC, the preferred interactive style of most coaches is a collaborative one, with coachees playing an active role. However, being flexible, CEB coaches are prepared to adopt a more challenging style with coachees looking to be challenged, and a didactic style with coachees looking for a greater instructional input from their coaches.

The more you can authentically modify your interactive style with different coachees, the greater number of coachees you are likely to help. Lazarus (1993) has referred to the coach who can genuinely modify their interactive style with different coachees as an "authentic chameleon".

Coach interactive styles may vary along a continuum rather than exist as either-or categories. The following are common style dimensions on which coaches may locate themselves:

- high activity – low activity
- formality – informality
- humour – seriousness
- uses self-disclosure – does not use self-disclosure.

As with other issues, the issue of your interactive style can be discussed by you and your coachee as part of the reflection process discussed earlier. It is also possible for you to get such information in questionnaire form from your coachees. Lazarus (1989) used several questions to assess clients' preferences concerning their therapists' interactive style in his Life History Questionnaire (LHQ). Modifying these for use in coaching we have the following:

- How do you think a coach should interact with his or her coachees?
- What personal qualities do you think the ideal coach should possess?

To this I might add the following:

- Which interactive style would you advise your coach to adopt if he or she were to get the most out of you as a coachee?
- Which interactive style would you advise your coach not to adopt when working with you and why?

3.1.4. The bonds of influence

In the 1980s, work emerging from social psychology in North America suggested that it was useful to consider the helping relationship as an interpersonal setting where influence takes place (Dorn, 1984). While not very popular among coachees, I have personally found it a useful way of thinking about why coachees listen to their coaches, independent of the message that the coach is trying to convey to them.

Coachees allow themselves to be influenced by you for three major reasons:

i) Because they like you or find you *attractive* in some way. I am not primarily thinking of physical attractiveness here, although this may be the case.
ii) Because they *trust* you (Gyllensten & Palmer, 2007; O'Broin & Palmer, 2010b).
iii) Because they are impressed by your *credibility* as a coach. This may include your expertise, experience and/or credentials. It may also be because they think you know what you are talking about because you have had personal experience of the problem for which your coachee is seeking help (in PF-CEBC) or of the objective towards which the coachee is striving (in DF-CEBC).

Taking this framework, it is possible to ask coachees the following question and be guided by their answer as part of the initial phase of coaching. "Are you most likely to listen to your coach and give credence to what they have to say, if you like the person, if you trust the person or if the person appears to know what they are talking about?" My view is that coaches should endeavour to meet their coachees' preferences on this matter to the extent that they are able to do so genuinely and to the extent that it is helpful for their coachees for them to do so.

Having considered the bonds of CEBC, in the next section I will consider a domain of the alliance that I introduced (Dryden, 2006, 2011): views.

3.2. Views in coaching

Views refer to the understandings that both participants have on salient issues. Effective CEBC, in my opinion, is based on several agreed understandings between you and your coachee. Disagreement over any facet of CEBC poses a threat to the coaching alliance and needs to be identified, discussed and resolved. This is only possible if you are both explicit about what you expect from yourself and your coachee during coaching. One of your major tasks, therefore, is to be explicit yourself and foster it in your coachee.

3.2.1. Negotiated consent

The heart of the views domain of the coaching alliance is a concept that I call negotiated consent. I have decided to use this term rather than the more usual term "informed consent" because it reflects the greater reality of you and your coachee negotiating important parts of the contract between you. The term "informed consent" means that your coachee is informed by you about relevant aspects of your coaching practice and, based on being informed, gives their consent to proceed with coaching. This seems to me to be a one-way process and does not allow for you, the coach, to be informed by what the coachee wants and for you to decide whether there are any elements that you disagree with and want to negotiate about. Based on this discussion and negotiation, you can choose to give your consent to proceed or to withhold it. The term "negotiated consent", therefore, better reflects the pluralistic nature of cognitive-emotive-behavioural coaching where the views of your coachee are taken very seriously and they are deemed to be an equal partner in the coaching process. From the coachee's perspective, if consent cannot be negotiated, then the coachee cannot be said to consent to the process and therefore coaching should not proceed, and if it does, then this practice would not generally be regarded as ethical.

I will now turn my attention to the issues you need to cover to which your coachee should be asked to give their consent. These are:

- the nature of coaching
- the nature of cognitive-emotive-behavioural approach to coaching and the roles and responsibilities of all interested parties

- confidentiality and its limits
- the practicalities of coaching.

Based on Garvin & Seabury's (1997) work, I make a distinction between an "enquirer", an "applicant" and a "coachee". When a person is in the enquiring role, they think they want coaching and are shopping around to see if they can decide about whether to seek coaching in a formal sense and, if so, how to find a suitable coach. When the person is in the applicant role, they have decided to seek coaching and have decided to have you as their coach. At this point, you need to discuss and negotiate several issues with them, at the end of which period if they give their consent to going forward based on a process of negotiation on these issues, they become your coachee, if you give your consent too.

3.2.1.1. The nature of coaching

It is important that you and the person seeking coaching help from you are in agreement about the nature of coaching and that coaching is best suited for what the coachee is seeking. In this book, as I have said, I am considering two forms of CEBC: development-focused CEBC and problem-focused CEBC. In the first, coaching is for people who are doing OK in life, but want more. They are looking to get more from themselves, from their work, from their relationships and from their lives. In the second, coaching is for people seeking help for practical or emotional problems in living.

3.2.1.1.1. WHEN COACHES HAVE EMOTIONAL PROBLEMS: THE INDICATIONS AND CONTRAINDICATIONS FOR EMOTIONAL PROBLEM-FOCUSED COACHING (EPF-C)

Cavanagh (2005), in an important chapter on mental health issues in executive coaching, outlined several guidelines to help coaches decide whether to offer coaching to executives in distress. I have used his guidelines to help coaches decide whether to offer applicants EPF-C for their emotional problems. I am writing this for those coaches who have been trained in both forms of coaching, but who do not have formal professional training in counselling/psychotherapy. Unless there is a good reason not to, I suggest that you make these points clear to an applicant so that you can have an open discussion on this issue.

1. *How long has the applicant been experiencing the emotional problem?*
   If the emotional problem is of recent origin or if it occurs intermittently, then EPF-C may be considered. However, if it occurs persistently or is chronic then EPF-C is not indicated and a judicious referral to a mental health specialist may be required.[4]

2. *How extreme are the responses of the applicant?*
   If the applicant's emotional, behavioural and/or thinking responses to the relevant adversity are distressing to the person, but lie within a mild to moderate range of distress, then EPF-C may be considered. However, if the applicant's distress is extreme then EPF-C is not indicated.
3. *How pervasive is the emotional problem?*
   If the applicant's emotional problem is limited to a certain situation or aspect of the person's life, then EPF-C may be considered. However, if it occurs in many situations and on many occasions then EPF-C is not indicated.
4. *How defensive is the applicant with respect to their emotional problem?*
   The applicant may meet the above three criteria with respect to the emotional problem for which they are seeking help, but still not be suitable for EPF-C because of their high level of defensiveness with respect to the problem. Signs of this include: a) actively seeking to avoid addressing the problem; b) being told by someone that they have to seek help and denying they have the problem themself; c) showing in their responses that they would struggle to cooperate with the coach when addressing the problem.
5. *How resistant to change is the emotional problem?*
   If it appears that the emotional problem is likely to persist despite the applicant's apparent willingness to address it, then this may indicate that the applicant is likely to have great difficulty in addressing the problem. While this can only really be judged once you and the applicant have decided to work together to address the problem in EPF-C (and when this occurs the applicant has become a coachee), if the person has failed to address the problem several times before in different ways, then this may be a contraindication for EPF-C. My advice here would be this. If the applicant's emotional problem is intermittent, non-pervasive, non-extreme and they indicate they can cooperate with you, then if their problem has seemed resistant to change in the past, offer to take them on if you can offer a fresh approach to the problem and one that makes sense to them and that they will agree to be referred to someone with more experience at dealing with the emotional problem than you if the problem continues to be resistant to change.

3.2.1.2. The nature of cognitive-emotive-behavioural coaching

Once you and the person have agreed that either development-focused coaching or problem-focused coaching is suitable for the person and you both want to proceed on that basis, you then need to explain the nature of CEBC so that the person applying for help can decide to proceed or not. This does not mean that you will give the person a lecture on the approach. What it means is that you will give the person some indication about what DF-CEBC or PF-CEBC is likely to entail for them and what they can reasonably expect from you.[5]

3.2.1.2.1. THE NATURE OF DF-CEBC

When you outline the nature of DF-CEBC, I suggest that you stress that your main role is initially to help the person to select areas of their life in which they wish to develop themself and to explain what CEBC says about the factors that need to be considered when this is done. Usually, you will help them to construct an action plan which will then guide the behaviours that they need to take to achieve their objective. Your main task, here, is to help them to adjust their behaviours based on their experiences in implementing the plan. If the person encounters an obstacle along the way and experiences a set of problematic responses to that obstacle, then you need to help them understand the cognitive-emotive-behavioural factors involved and then deal with them. In helping the person deal with their problematic responses to the encountered obstacle you have moved from practising DF-CEBC to EPF-CEBC and it is useful to make this clear to the person applying for coaching help that this might happen and to reiterate this when it happens as the nature of the coaching contract may have changed.

It is also important to point out to the person seeking your help that although you have a CEB perspective on what they discuss with you, you are also flexible and pluralistic in approach and will seek and incorporate the person's own perspective when agreeing a shared view on their objectives and on which concepts these objectives should be based.

3.2.1.2.2. THE NATURE OF PROBLEM-FOCUSED CEBC

When you outline the nature of PF-CEBC, you need to explain the difference between a practical problem and an emotional problem.

A practical problem is one where your coachee is confused, tangled up with an issue or issues and needs clarity and order, which they hope to get by talking things through with someone, but they are not emotionally disturbed about the issue(s). If your coachee has a practical problem, you need to help your coachee adopt a problem-solving approach. An example of such an approach has been provided by Palmer (2008), who has outlined a model he calls PRACTICE (see page 56). I will refer to this sub-type of problem-focused cognitive-emotive-behavioural coaching as *practical problem-focused cognitive-emotive-behavioural coaching* (PPF-CEBC).[6]

An emotional problem is one where the person has an emotionally disturbed reaction to an adversity. Here you need to stress that you will help the person first understand the problem using a cognitive-emotive-behavioural framework and how they unwittingly maintain it by employing a range of CEB factors. Then you will help them address the relevant problematic cognitions and unconstructive behaviours so that they can deal with the adversity in a healthy manner. However, again it is important that you make clear that you are flexible and pluralistic in your coaching practice and that you will seek and incorporate the person's own perspective on these matters when agreeing a shared view of their problem and what they need to do to deal with it effectively. I will refer to this sub-type of problem-focused cognitive-emotive-behavioural coaching as *emotional problem-focused cognitive-emotive-behavioural coaching* (EPF-CEBC).[7]

3.2.1.2.2.1. Examples of problems dealt with in PF-CEBC. Here are examples of coachees' problems in living (both practical and emotional) that coaches have indicated in their promotional material that they have dealt with in PF-CEBC. They can thus be indications for PF-CEBC. Thus, in a work context, one cognitive-behavioural coaching website[8] lists the following issues for which they claim their coachees have sought help and successfully dealt with using coaching:

- Managing challenging situations with colleagues / bosses / clients
- Managing underperformance
- Managing excessive workload / managing stress
- Dealing with fear of failure (and success)
- Managing conflicting demands of work and personal life
- Fear of public speaking / giving presentations
- Desire to be more assertive / improve personal impact
- Coping with redundancy.

In a personal CEBC context, another website[9] says that coaching (or what I am calling here problem-focused coaching or PF-CEBC) seeks to help coachees to:

- Become more assertive with friends and family
- Tackle people and situations that they have avoided
- Overcome a personal block such as taking up a healthier lifestyle. Other blocks might include stress, confidence issues, overcoming negative thinking, perfectionism and dealing with work-related difficulties.

3.2.1.3. The roles and responsibilities of all stakeholders

In life coaching, where a person seeks help from you as a coach in independent practice for work and/or non-work issues, then the two of you are the main stakeholders in the work (Grant & Cavanagh, 2010). This is the case particularly when the person is responsible for paying for their own coaching. When the person is being funded by someone else (e.g. their employing organisation), this generally means that this someone else has a stake in the person's coaching (and is thus a stakeholder) and has roles and responsibilities that need to be clarified. It is important, therefore, that you and your potential coachee are clear about what these roles and responsibilities are and to what extent any stakeholders are to be involved in coaching and what the nature of that involvement is.

3.2.1.4. Confidentiality and its limits

Like other forms of helping, coaching cannot be completely confidential, and as such, you need to state clearly, and preferably in writing, what are the exceptions to complete confidentiality. Confidentiality with respect to internal coaching is more complex than with respect to external coaching and I refer you to Iordanou, Hawley, & Iordanou (2017) for a full discussion of this issue and other issues pertaining to confidentiality.

3.2.1.5. The practicalities of CEBC

The fifth area of coaching that you need to be clear about at the outset concerns what might be called the practicalities of coaching. From a coaching alliance perspective, what is important here is that both you and your coachee are clear concerning what to expect from one another in each of the following areas and that you agree with each other with respect to these expectations. These include:

- The length and frequency of coaching sessions and the duration of coaching
- The medium of coaching (e.g. face-to-face; Skype)
- Your fee, how it is to be paid and who is responsible for paying it
- Your cancellation policy
- Coach–coachee contact outside formal coaching sessions.

3.2.2. Views on coachee problems and obstacles

From the perspective of the coaching alliance, it is very important that you and your coachee agree on what problem(s) you are both going to address in problem-focused CEBC, what obstacles you are both going to tackle in both PF-CEBC and DF-CEBC[10] and how these problems and obstacles can be understood. This involves using the CEBC framework that you previously outlined in general and applying it to the specific problem(s) that your coachee wishes to address.

3.2.3. Views on the CEBC approach to be taken with your coachee

Earlier in this chapter, I mentioned that it is important for you to explain CEBC to the person seeking coaching from you so that the two of you can discuss whether coaching along the lines of CEBC is what the person is looking for and whether it is suitable to them. Such a discussion is informed by the person's own ideas about the kind of coaching they are looking for. If an agreement can be reached, negotiated consent is given by both parties to proceed. This agreement on the type of coaching to be offered to the person is done at a *general* level.

However, when you have discovered what the coachee is looking for either with respect to their development-based objectives or their problem-based goals, you can outline, in more *specific* terms, the coaching approach that you propose to take. From a pluralistic perspective, it is important that you elicit your coachee's ideas of what coaching approach they are looking for and then negotiate a way forward based on your respective inputs.

3.2.3.1. Views on the DF-CEBC/PF-CEBC approach negotiated with your coachee

Here, I will assume that you and your coachee know what the latter wants to achieve from coaching and that you have helped them to select a target objective in DF-CEBC and a target problem/goal to work towards in PF-CEBC. At this point, you need to do three things (the order of the first two is as seems most appropriate):

1. Tell your coachee how you intend to help them based on your specific approach to coaching. In PF-CEBC, if your coachee has a practical problem, explain practical problem-focused CEBC and if they have an emotional problem, explain emotional problem-focused CEBC.
2. Encourage your coachee to share their view on the best way they can be coached on their objective/goal.
3. Discuss these two views and negotiate an agreed way forward.

In the next section, I will discuss the raison d'être of CEB coaching: its purpose.

3.3. Objectives/goals in CEBC

Goals/objectives refer to the purpose of the coaching meetings. In this book, I use the following terminology. I use the term "goals" when writing about the aims of problem-focused CEBC and the term "objectives" when writing about the aims of development-focused CEBC.[11]

3.3.1. Agreeing development-based objectives in CEBC

The main task that you have in the objective alliance domain of development-focused CEBC (DF-CEBC) is to help your coachee set as many development-based objectives as they want in a variety of life areas, but, when doing so, you both need to be mindful of how many sessions you have contracted for.

3.3.1.1. Development-based objectives in CEBC: achievement, maintenance and enhancement

Once objectives are achieved, they should be maintained and, if relevant, enhanced. You need to be aware of these related issues as you help your coachee work towards their objectives.

3.3.1.2. Maximising the chances that your coachee will achieve their development-based objectives

When discussing your coachee's objectives with them, it is useful to have in mind several points that will inform the selection of these objectives. These are the foundations that maximise the chances that your coachee will persist in their development-related work. Consider the following points:

- Help your coachee set a clear objective. The clearer the objective, the more likely it is that your coachee will achieve them.
- Help your coachee set a development-based objective that is one that your coachee truly wants to achieve (Gessnitzer & Kauffeld, 2015). I call this objective an "intrinsic objective" to contrast it with an extrinsic objective, which is what someone else wants your coachee to achieve.
- Help your coachee select an objective that is based on a core value.
- If your coachee values social support, help them to identify those who may support them as they work towards their objective.
- Help your coachee select an objective that can be integrated into their life once achieved.
- Help your coachee to select an objective for which they are prepared to make sacrifices.

3.3.2. Agreeing problem-based goals in coaching

The main task that you have in the goal-alliance domain of problem-focused coaching (PF-CEBC)[12] is to help your coachee set a goal with respect to each of the problems for which they are seeking help. Again, in doing this, you need to be mindful of how many sessions you have contracted for.

3.3.2.1. The nature of problem-based goals

As I discussed earlier, when your coachee has a problem for which they are seeking coaching, this may be because a) they are confused, tangled up with an issue or issues and need clarity and order which they hope to get by talking things through with someone, but they are not emotionally disturbed about the issue(s) – I call this a practical problem – or b) they have an emotionally disturbed response to an adversity and their behaviour is unconstructive – I call this an emotional problem. With a practical problem, it is important that you help your coachee be specific about what would constitute the solution to the problem. With an emotional problem, it is important that you help the person deal with the adversity in a constructive way, both emotionally and behaviourally. Explain why facing and dealing with the adversity is important and why bypassing the adversity won't work in the longer term.

3.3.2.2. Problem-based goals: achievement and maintenance

Once your coachee has achieved their goal, they still need to continue to do some work to maintain their gains. Once they feel confident that they can do this maintenance work on their own you can then switch to targeting another of their problems and set a suitable goal with respect to this new target problem.

3.3.2.3. Maximising the chances that your coachee will achieve their problem-based goals

In the previous section, I dealt with several factors that would increase the chances that your coachee would achieve their development-based objectives and I refer you to that discussion. A number of those factors are also relevant when helping your coachee to achieve their goals. In particular:

- The clearer your coachee can be about what they want to achieve with respect to their problem, then the more likely they are to achieve it and/or to maintain it once achieved.
- Help your coachee to set an intrinsic goal (what they truly want to achieve), not an extrinsic one (what another person wants them to achieve).
- Encourage them to set up a support system, if they think such social support will be useful in helping them to achieve their goals(s).
- Help your coachee to select a goal for which they are prepared to make sacrifices.

3.4. Tasks in CEBC

Tasks refer to the procedures carried out by both coach and coachee in the service of the latter's goals/objectives. From an alliance perspective, the following issues become salient:

1. Help your coachee understand that they have coaching tasks to perform and that they know the nature of these tasks.
2. Help your coachee see that performing their tasks will help them to achieve their objectives/goals.
3. Help your coachee understand that they need to work to change.

4. Assess your coachee's capability to carry out the coaching tasks required of them. If they have the capability, proceed with these tasks, but if they do not have the capability, suggest that they use different tasks, ones that they can execute.
5. Assess whether your coachee has the necessary skills to carry out the coaching tasks required of them. If they do not have the skills, then train them in these skills yourself if you are able to do so or help them to source someone who can offer such training if you are not.
6. Help your coachee to develop the confidence to execute the relevant tasks. You can do this in three ways:
   - Help your coachee practise the task in the coaching session until they feel confident to do the tasks on their own.
   - Encourage them to join a relevant group or organisation that specialises in teaching the skill where they can learn and practise it until they gain confidence.
   - Encourage your coachee to carry out the task unconfidently, pointing out that confidence comes from undertaking an activity and is rarely experienced before the activity is first attempted.
7. Ensure that the task has sufficient potency to facilitate objective/goal achievement.
8. Refrain from using tasks or suggesting that your coachee uses tasks that may serve to perpetuate their problems.
9. Help your coachee understand the nature of your tasks as coach and how these relate to their tasks as coachee and to their development-based objectives and/or problem-based goals.
10. Ensure that your coachee is in a sufficiently good frame of mind to execute their tasks.

3.4.1. Tasks and your expertise as a coach

Your effectiveness as a coach is partly dependent on your expertise as a practitioner. I say partly here, because no matter how expert you are in carrying out your coaching tasks, unless your coachee carries out their tasks then coaching will not be effective. Here is a sample of issues that pertain to your expertise in executing your tasks.

3.4.1.1. Coach skill

From a coaching alliance perspective, the degree to which your coachee makes progress may be due in some measure to the skill with which you perform your tasks as coach. If you are skilful in the execution of your tasks, you increase the chances that your clients will have confidence in your ability and see you as being helpful (Pinsof & Catherall, 1986). However, it is important that you realise that you develop skill as a coach gradually and that if you want to be competent as a coaching practitioner you need to accept moving from a state of conscious incompetence to conscious competence and hence to unconscious competence. This will require ongoing supervision of your coaching practice.

3.4.1.2. Explaining your coaching approach and gaining negotiated consent

I mentioned earlier that, from a coaching alliance perspective, it is important that your coachee understands your coaching approach so that they can give what I have called "negotiated consent"[13] before you both embark on the coaching process. Not only is negotiating consent an ethical position, it is also good practice. For giving negotiated consent indicates that your coachee understands your coaching approach, has had an opportunity to suggest modifications to it and is actively choosing to involve themself in the coaching process after a period of negotiation.

It follows from this that there are four core skills that you need to develop to a high level of competence. These are (i) explaining CEBC to a variety of different coachees; ii) eliciting your coachee's preferences about the coaching approach they wish to receive; iii) discussing any differences and negotiating an approach to which you both can commit; and (iv) gaining negotiated consent.

3.4.1.3. Making judicious referrals

It is important to realise that not everyone who seeks coaching from you will be suitable for that help. This may be the case for several reasons. First, they may be looking for a different type of help. For example, some people come for coaching for advice on how to change others and are not interested in looking at their own contribution to their relationships. Second, the person applying for your help may be suitable for coaching, but may want a very different approach to CEBC. Third, the person may be seeking coaching, may be suitable for the approach to coaching that you practise, but you consider that you may not be the best person to see them. Thus, the person may be better helped by a coach of the same gender as themself but different from yours, or they may be better helped by someone who has a different personality type to you. Furthermore, your coachee may be seeking a specific type of coaching which requires specialist knowledge or skills that you don't possess, but you know a colleague who does possess that knowledge or those skills.

It follows from the above that determining the best type of help for the people who have come to see you and making a judicious referral if necessary are core skills that you need to develop as a coach. It is particularly important when you make a referral that you inspire the person with the hope that the coach to whom you are referring them is the best person to offer the most appropriate help.

3.4.1.4. Varying your use of coaching tasks

A theme that has run through this chapter, albeit implicitly, is that since coachees differ (along several key dimensions), coaches need to vary their own contribution to the coaching process. This has clear implications for coachee objectives and/or goals since there is more than one way to help your coachee, and if one set of coach tasks is not helpful to particular coachees than others may be.

A useful system – known as Thinking-Feeling-Action (TFA) – that is relevant to the variation of coach tasks was devised by Hutchins (1984). He argued that coaches can improve the effectiveness of coaching they have with their coachees by varying the tasks they use with different clients. Here they should strive to focus on tasks that match their coachee's predominant modes (thinking, feeling or action) unless there is a good reason to help coachees focus on their non-preferred modes.

While Hutchins focuses on the client's predominant modes of dealing with the world, he makes the point that coaches also have similar predominant modes. While in an ideal world effective coaches would, with equal facility, be able to use cognitive, behavioural and affective tasks, the fact that coaches have their own limitations means that it is a temptation for them to restrict themselves to using tasks which reflect their predominant orientation (cognitive, emotive or behavioural). Hutchins's (1984) analysis implies that should coaches restrict themselves to using particular intervention modes (that is, cognitive, emotive or behavioural), they would help a smaller range of coachees than if they became more flexible in freely and appropriately using cognitive, emotive and behavioural tasks. It follows from this that to increase their effectiveness in the task domain of the alliance, coaches need to acknowledge their own task preferences and work on broadening their own range of task behaviour – a task which itself calls for continual exposure to what coaching models other than their own preferred model have to offer – a project which is consistent with the flexible and pluralistic nature of CEBC as outlined in this book.

3.4.1.5. Capitalising on the coachee's learning style

As used here, coaching tasks (broadly conceptualised) are how coachees achieve their development-based objectives and/or problem-based goals. If coachees do achieve their objectives/goals it is because they have learned something new (for example, to see things differently and/or to act differently).

Taking a coaching alliance perspective on coachee learning, you need to consider how best to facilitate such learning for each of your coachees. For example, you need to discover how each of your coachees learns best and capitalise on this by tailoring your interventions accordingly.

3.4.1.6. Helping your coachee to get the most out of their coaching tasks

Given the fact that your coachee has tasks to carry out in coaching, however specifically or broadly these tasks are conceived, what should you do to help your coachee get the most out of these tasks? Here is a selection of possible interventions:

1. Negotiate with your coachee what their tasks are.
2. Help your coachee see clearly the relationship between their tasks and their coaching objectives and/or goals. Encourage them to keep this connection clearly in mind during coaching.
3. Modify these tasks after considering your coachee's strengths and weaknesses. You can do this both before your coachee carries out their tasks and after they have done so. In the latter case, you can modify the tasks based on your coachee's feedback on their attempts to use them.
4. Train your coachee in these tasks if relevant.
5. Problem-solve any obstacles to coachee task execution.
6. Have alternative coachee tasks in mind if your coachee does not want to or cannot carry out their original tasks.
7. When negotiating homework assignments with your coachee, make sure that they specify what they are going to do, when they are going to do it and how often. Problem-solve possible obstacles to homework completion.

3.4.1.7. Using different tasks in the two different types of CEBC

I have made a distinction between two different types of CEBC: problem-focused CEBC (PF-CEBC), where your coachee comes to see you because they have a problem (or problems) for which they seek help, and development-focused CEBC (DF-CEBC), where your coachee comes to see you because they wish to get more out of themselves, their career and/or their personal life. These different types of coaching do require different tasks. Broadly speaking, in DF-CEBC your tasks, and that of your coachee, are focused on the promotion of the coachee's development and growth. In practical problem-focused CEBC (PPF-CEBC), your respective tasks are mainly to help your coachee gain greater clarity on the issues that they are facing so that they can problem-solve more effectively, while in emotional problem-focused coaching (EPF-CEBC) your respective tasks are focused on helping your coachee deal healthily with adversity. Difficulties occur in coaching where coaches use and suggest that coachees use tasks that are not appropriate for the type of coaching they have both contracted for, but are more appropriate for the other type of coaching. The issue for coaches who are primarily counsellors and therapists is that they tend to be more comfortable working with emotional problems and thus there is a tendency to want to practise EPF-CEBC; and the issue for coaches who are primarily trained as coaches is that they tend to flounder when faced with coachees' emotional problems. This is why the compleat coach is equally at home with both types of coaching and can move with ease from the one type to the other.

3.4.1.8. Using tasks at different stages of CEBC

It is likely that your tasks as coach and your coachee's tasks will change during the coaching process. From a coaching alliance perspective, it is important that you both understand this and feel able to refer the matter to the reflection process if you need to discuss it.

3.4.1.8.1. HOW YOUR COACHING TASKS CHANGE OVER TIME IN CEBC

The main change in your CEB coaching tasks over time is that at the beginning of coaching you will be probably quite active in the process. As coaching progresses, your level of activity will decrease as you will encourage your coachee to take greater responsibility for their coaching and carry out some of the tasks that you initiated earlier in the process, so that towards the end you will become more of a consultant than a coach. This means that you will prompt your coachee when they falter at self-coaching rather than take more of an active interventionist role.

In what follows, I list your coaching tasks roughly in the order that you will carry them out to give you a sense of how your tasks vary over time. During coaching, you will do such things as:

- Determine whether the person seeking help is a good candidate for coaching and, if so, which type of coaching is most appropriate
- Negotiate consent with your coachee
- Introduce the concept of the reflection process and explain how it works. Initiate this process as appropriate
- Help your coachee to set development-based objectives or problem-based goals
- Discuss with your coachee which tasks they are able and willing to do in order to achieve their objective and/or goal
- Help your coachee to plan to carry out their tasks
- Encourage them to initiate and maintain this action plan
- Train your coachee to use skills that they can use, but that are not currently in their skills repertoire
- Discuss how their action plan needs to be altered based on their experiences of task execution

- Help your coachee to anticipate potential obstacles and intervene so that they don't become actual obstacles
- Help your coachee to identify and deal with any actual obstacles that do occur
- Once your coachee has achieved their objectives and/or goals, help them to maintain and extend their gains within the specified life area or problem to other life areas or problems
- Develop an agreed plan with your coachee to end coaching
- Set up agreed follow-up sessions.

3.4.1.8.2. HOW YOUR COACHEE'S TASKS CHANGE OVER TIME IN CEBC

Your coachee's tasks also change over time. While effective coaching is characterised by your coachee's active involvement in the process, as pointed out above, as coaching unfolds you will become more of a consultant to the change process and they will assume increasingly greater responsibility for managing their own change.

In what follows, I list your coachee's tasks again roughly in the order that they will carry them out to give you a sense of how their tasks vary over time. During coaching, your coachee will be expected to do such things as:

- Inform you of where they are in their life and where they would like to be in DF-CEBC (i.e. set objectives) and what their problems are and what help they are looking for with respect to these problems in PF-CEBC (i.e. set goals)
- Give consent to proceed after a period of negotiation
- Initiate the reflection process as appropriate
- Give honest reactions to your suggestions about how you would approach coaching with them and on other matters
- Give their suggestions about what would be helpful to them in coaching
- Engage with you in developing an action plan with respect to their objectives and/or goals
- Initiate and maintain the tasks specified in the action plan and be prepared to modify the plan in response to their experiences of carrying out agreed tasks
- Predict and deal with potential obstacles
- Disclose and deal with actual obstacles
- Work out a plan with you to maintain and enhance gains
- Work out a plan to end coaching
- Engage in agreed follow-up sessions.

In the following chapter, I will deal with the issues that arise when someone seeks you out for coaching. In particular, I will discuss how to determine a) whether they are suitable for coaching; b) whether they are suitable for cognitive-emotive-behavioural coaching; and if so, c) which type of CEBC will best suit them at the outset.

Notes

1 Currently often referred to as "respect".
2 I prefer the term "acceptance" to "unconditional positive regard" or "respect".
3 George Kelly was the originator of personal construct psychology.
4 In this section, please assume that whenever I say that PF-C may not be indicated, I suggest that the coach refers the person to a suitable mental health specialist.
5 By "your specific approach", I don't just mean what school of coaching you are most closely associated with, but what distinguishes your approach. This may be an eclectic, integrative or pluralistic approach. Whatever it is, you need to explain this to your coachee.
6 Some problems may have practical and emotional components. This issue lies outside of the scope of this book.
7 Some problems may have practical and emotional components. This issue lies outside of the scope of this book.
8 www.cbtoxford.com/cbt-coaching-oxford-companies-groups as of 22/12/16.
9 www.cognitivebehaviouralcoachingworks.com/individual-coaching-services/ as of 22/12/16.
10 See the discussion on obstacles below.
11 I also use the term "goals" to refer to what the person wants to achieve in addressing the obstacles to the pursuit of their development-based objectives or problem-based goals.
12 When discussing goals in this section, I refer to goals with respect to problems in PF-C, as noted, and goals with respect to actual obstacles in DF-C.
13 If you recall, I prefer the term "negotiated consent" to the more traditional "informed consent". In the latter, the coachee is passive. They are informed by the coach and then they either give their consent, or they do not. In the former, the coachee is active. They are informed by the coach, but they also inform the coach about their preferences and give their consent, or not, after a period of negotiation.

Chapter 4

Greeting, assessing and contracting

In this chapter, I will discuss how to initiate the process of cognitive-emotive-behavioural coaching. It is important to get CEBC off on the right footing so I will discuss how to respond when someone first gets in contact with you.

4.1. Remember the distinctions between "enquirer", "applicant" and "coachee" roles in coaching

In Chapter 3, I introduced you to the work of Garvin & Seabury (1997), who distinguished between an "applicant" and a "client" in interpersonal social work. Drawing on this distinction, I have found it useful to add the role of "enquirer" and to ask myself which role a person occupies when they first make contact: are they in the "enquirer" role or the "applicant" role? It is important to note that when a person first makes contact they cannot be in the "coachee" role as they have not given their consent to anything.

Be mindful of these distinctions as you greet your coachee and assess why they have come to see you. Let me give a brief definition of each role as I will use them in this book.

4.1.1. The enquirer role

When someone is in the "enquirer" role they are making enquiries about coaching. They may have little idea of what they are looking for and are hoping that their initial enquiries will prompt their thinking in this regard. On the other hand, they may have a clear idea about what kind of coaching they are looking for, but are shopping around for a particular coach who may be most useful to them and/or who may give them the best "deal".

4.1.2. The applicant role

When someone is in the "applicant" role they have made a decision to seek coaching and to seek it from you. However, they don't know yet what working with you would involve and you don't know whether a) you are the best person to help them, or b) if you can help them.

4.1.3. The coachee role

When the person seeking your help becomes your coachee, you have both agreed on the type of coaching to which the person is best suited, you both think that you can help the person and you are both in agreement concerning the practicalities of coaching. In other words, you have both negotiated and given consent to proceed.

4.2. Greeting the person

These days a person may contact you in a number of ways, but in my view it is a good idea to talk with the person on the phone (or by Skype) as soon as possible so you can have a real-time conversation with them.[1] Ultimately, this will save you and the person contacting you much time in the long run. This does not mean that you should spend a long time speaking with the person, but a 10-minute conversation will help you both to conclude that you are *not* the right coach for the person or that it is worthwhile to schedule a face-to-face meeting because you *may be* the right coach.

4.2.1. The brief, real-time conversation

When you speak to the person in real time, I suggest you ask some (or all) of the following questions. As you do so, you will need to be quite focused and prepared to take the lead in the conversation.

4.2.1.1. "What are you looking for?"

If the person mentions that they are looking for help that is *not* covered by the following then it is clear that you cannot be their coach:

- Your coachee is confused, tangled up with an issue or issues and needs clarity and order, which they hope to get by talking things through with someone, but they are not emotionally disturbed about the issue(s). This is indicative for coaching for practical problems (see Chapters 5 and 6).
- Your coachee has an emotional problem where the person has an emotionally disturbed reaction to an adversity (see Chapters 7 and 8).
- Your coachee wishes to develop themself in one or more areas of their life (see Chapters 9 and 10).

4.2.1.2. "Who suggested that you contact me and why?"

It may be that the person has been misinformed about your services by the referring person. It is important to explain this so that the person can search elsewhere for what they are looking for.

4.2.1.3. "Are you looking for ongoing coaching or a time-limited contract? If the latter, how much time or how many sessions are you thinking of?"

It is useful to know, at the outset, about the person's view of how much time they can commit to coaching. In particular, if they want to achieve a lot in a very short period of time, this might be problematic. I have written a book on what might be realistically achieved from very brief coaching of between one and three sessions (Dryden, 2017).

4.2.1.4. "Who will be funding your coaching?"

If the person is funding themself this is different from the situation where the person is being funded. It is useful to have such knowledge because if the person is not funding their own coaching, the sponsor may have expectations of you, as coach, which you need to discuss with the person. If I am going to meet the person again for a formal, assessment-based session and I know that they are going to be sponsored, I ask them to find out what the sponsor's expectations are with respect to any involvement in their coaching before I see them. Then I can discuss this more fully as part of contracting.

4.2.1.5. "My fee is £... per session. Is this acceptable to you or the person funding your coaching?"

It saves everybody time if the person or their funder knows your fee. There is no point in continuing if your fee is outside the financial reach of the feepayer, taking into account some room for flexibility.

4.2.1.6. "Is there anything important you would like to tell me at this stage?"

Before deciding whether to invite the person to a face-to-face assessment session, it is important to give them an opportunity to tell you any information that they think you need to know at this stage. This information may or may not affect your decision to invite the person to a face-to-face assessment session.

4.2.1.7. Decision time

After you have a spoken to the person for about ten minutes, you should be clear if the person is looking for a service that you cannot provide. If so, you should tell them honestly and kindly and provide them with an appropriate referral if you are able. If you think that you may be able to help the person, then tell them so, but stress that you will need to meet them for an hour to carry out a fuller assessment, to discuss the practicalities of coaching and to answer any questions that they may have about the process before you

Greeting, assessing and contracting 49

both make a joint decision to work together. At this point, formal contracting takes place.

Some coaches offer the first session free and therefore, if this is not the case with you, it is important to state that you charge for the assessment session at your normal rate (if this is the case).

4.3. Assessing the person for CEBC

In the brief, real-time conversation you had with the person (see above), I suggested that you ask the person what they are looking for, the purpose of which was to identify any requests for your coaching help that were inappropriate or unsuitable. When you meet the person face-to-face for an assessment session your purpose is different. It is to find out which type of cognitive-emotive-behavioural coaching (CEBC) might be most appropriate for the person. You need this information to help with the contracting period that comes after this initial assessment. Although I have mentioned this earlier in this chapter and in Chapter 3, I present here the major criterion for each type of CEB coaching discussed in this book.

4.3.1. Criteria for the different types of CEBC

In the situation where the person seeking coaching has *either* a practical problem, an emotional problem *or* seeks to develop themselves, then the following criteria are relevant.

- For practical problem-focused CEBC (PPF-CEBC)

Your coachee is confused, tangled up with an issue or issues and needs clarity and order, which they hope to get by talking things through with someone, but they are not emotionally disturbed about the issue(s).

- For emotional problem-focused CEBC (EPF-CEBC)

Your coachee has an emotional problem or problems where the person has an emotionally disturbed reaction to an adversity.

- For development-focused CEBC (DF-CEBC)

Your coachee wishes to develop themself in one or more areas of their life.

4.3.2. When the person's coaching requirements are more complex

So far, I have assumed that your coachee is looking for help with *one* of the following: i) a practical problem or problems; ii) an emotional problem or problems; or iii) a wish to develop themself in one or more life areas. However, what if the person wants help in two or all three areas?

When this happens, you can do one of three things.

1. Suggest to the person that you can help them in the following order: i) their emotional problem(s);[2] ii) their practical problem(s); iii) their wish to develop themself. In doing so, you can explain that when someone has an emotional problem then this tends to preoccupy them so that they can't concentrate on their practical problems as much as they could if they were free from this problem. Also, if someone has a practical problem (but no emotional problem) then this preoccupation is present, but to a lesser extent. It is only when the person is not facing an emotional problem or a practical problem that they can concentrate fully on developing themself.
2. Ask the person in which order they think it is best for them to tackle their problems/developmental issues.
3. Do a combination of 2 and 3 and then refer any differences in approach to the reflection process for discussion and decision.

4.4. Contracting with the person

For you both to have reached the contracting phase of coaching, you and the person seeking your help have agreed that you are the best person to help them with the issue or issues for which they are seeking help and you have agreed on the best type of CEBC that is suited to the issue(s). If the person has mixed reasons for seeking coaching, you have also agreed the order in which these different issues will be tackled.

4.4.1. Negotiating consent

I have already discussed the concept of negotiated consent in Chapter 3. If you will recall, I prefer the term "negotiated consent" to the more traditional "informed consent". In the latter, the coachee is passive. They are informed by the coach and then they either give their consent, or they do not. In the former, the coachee is active. They are informed by the coach, but they also inform the coach about their preferences and give their consent, or not, after a period of negotiation. Thus, when you and your coachee discuss your contract it is done within the spirit of negotiating consent.

4.4.2. The content of the contract

Most coaches use a written contract. What topics should ideally form part of such a contract? In my view the following:

- The start of the contract and the end of the contract, if known
- The type of coaching contracted for
- The approach to coaching that you, as coach, take
- Your fees and how they are to be paid
- Any between-session contacts between you and your coachee and how they will be charged for
- Your cancellation policy
- Confidentiality and its exceptions
- The roles and responsibilities of you, as coach, and your coachee
- Your referral policy
- Any other items to be agreed by you and your coachee.

I have discussed many of these topics already in Chapters 2 and 3 and you should consult these chapters for this information. The one issue that I have not discussed in full elsewhere, which I will mention here, covers your referral policy.

4.4.2.1. Your referral policy

Your referral policy should state the conditions under which you would suggest referring your coachee to another professional. These might include:

4.4.2.1.1. YOUR COACHEE'S PROBLEMS ARE BEYOND YOUR LEVEL OF EXPERTISE

Cavanagh (2005) argues that there are a number of contraindications for what I call here emotional problem-focused CEBC (EPF-CEBC). These are:

i) when your coachee's emotional problem occurs persistently or is chronic;
ii) when it is pervasive;
iii) when your coachee's level of distress is extreme;
iv) when they show a high level of defensiveness with respect to their problem; and/or
v) when the emotional problem is likely to be resistant to change.

While you may have the expertise to deal with your coachee's emotional problem under more benign conditions,[3] the level of expertise needed to help your coachee with their emotional problem under these more challenging conditions exceeds yours and you need to refer the person to a professional who has the required level of expertise. This will usually be a psychotherapist or a clinical psychologist, but sometimes it may be a psychiatrist. It needs be added that this should preferably occur before a contract has been made, but sometimes the coachee initially downplays the severity of their problem.

In addition, while you may have the level of expertise to deal with your coachee's initial emotional problem, they may have a subsequent problem or problems which may require a higher level of expertise than you have.

4.4.2.1.2. YOU LACK THE SPECIALIST EXPERTISE TO HELP YOUR COACHEE

While in the above scenario you have relevant expertise, but not at the required level to help your coachee, it may occur that during the process of coaching your coachee requires some input from someone who has specialist expertise that you lack. For example, such a person may be an expert in career development or have expertise in the field of business in which your coachee works. Here you can refer your coachee to such a person and continue to coach them at the same time, or you can stop coaching the person and perhaps restart if and when your coachee requests this later.

4.4.3. The organic nature of the coaching contract

While a written and signed contract between you and your coachee is important in that it makes clear to both of you what is likely to happen in coaching and what you can realistically and explicitly expect of one another, it is not set in stone. Indeed, in my view the contract reflects the dynamic process of coaching itself. While some of the clauses in the contract are unlikely to change (e.g. confidentiality, your fees and your cancellation policy), others may be added or are liable to change.

4.4.3.1. Additions to and deletions from the contract

I mentioned at the beginning of the chapter that a person becomes your coachee when they have given what I call "negotiated consent" to proceed. At this point, you have a contract with them and I have outlined above the items that are likely to be in the contract. One of these items pertains to the type of coaching contracted for: practical problem-focused CEBC; emotional problem-focused CEBC; and development-focused CEBC. However, while you and your coachee will know what type of coaching you both have contracted for, you will not know in detail, at the contracting stage, what problem(s) your coachee is seeking help for in PF-CEBC or in what ways they want to develop themself in DF-CEBC. This information will only become apparent when you have developed a working relationship and begun the work of coaching. Contracting, as I conceive it, is the foundation for coaching, but what transpires in coaching means that some additional foundations need to be laid.

With this in mind, in problem-focused CEBC (PF-CEBC), when you and your coachee have identified the latter's problems for which they are seeking help and have set goals with respect to these problems, then this information could be added to the contract. Similarly, in development-focused CEBC (DF-CEBC), when you and your coachee have set development-based objectives, then these can be added to the contract. Every time your coachee adds a problem/goal or a development to the agenda of coaching, this could be added to the contract. Similarly when you have helped your coach to address a problem and achieve the related goal or when you have helped them to achieve a development-based objective then the appropriate deletions from the contract can be made

4.4.3.2. Changes to the contract

As well as adding items to the contract as discussed above, it is important for you and your coachee to bear in mind that you can make agreed changes to the contract, again reflecting the dynamic nature of coaching. Here are some examples of agreed changes being made to a coaching contract.

4.4.3.2.1. CHANGES TO THE CONTENT OF YOUR COACHEE'S PROBLEM(S) AND PROBLEM-RELATED GOAL(S) THAT ALREADY APPEAR IN THE CONTRACT

It sometimes occurs in problem-focused coaching that a problem that your coachee is seeking help for turns out to be different in nature (either wholly or in part) than you both originally thought and this change needs to be reflected in the coaching contract along with any change to the related goal.

4.4.3.2.2. CHANGES TO THE CONTENT OF YOUR COACHEE'S DEVELOPMENT-BASED OBJECTIVE(S)

Similarly, it sometimes occurs that your coachee realises that what they thought they wanted to achieve with respect to developing themself in a particular life area, and that they had contracted for, turns out to be different from what they originally thought. In which case, an appropriate modification to the contract needs to be made.

4.4.3.2.3. CHANGES TO THE TYPE OF COACHING CONTRACTED FOR

When your coachee has effectively dealt with their practical problem(s) or emotional problem(s), then they may be interested in contracting with you for DF-CEBC where the focus is on developing themself in one or more areas of their life. If so, you would need to modify the coaching contract accordingly.

4.4.3.2.4. CHANGES TO YOUR AND/OR YOUR COACHEE'S ROLES AND RESPONSIBILITIES

Any negotiated changes to your roles and responsibilities and/or those of your coachee should be marked by the appropriate changes to the contract if the original contract was not broad enough to assimilate these changes.

4.4.3.2.5. CHANGES TO THE DURATION OF THE COACHING CONTRACT

Unless you have contracted with your coachee for a fixed number of sessions or a fixed time period, both of which cannot be modified, then it is likely that your original contract with respect to the duration of coaching will need to be modified to reflect changes in how long you have decided to work together. Such changes can reflect either the lengthening or the shortening of the contract to reflect what has happened during coaching.

Having discussed the foundations of coaching in this chapter, in the following chapters I will discuss the three types of CEBC, beginning with practical problem-focused CEBC in the next chapter.

Notes

1 In Chapter 6, I provide an extended example of the greeting, assessing and contracting process with a person seeking help for a practical problem. This will show how a CEB coach approaches this tripartite task and is broadly similar in EPF-CEBC and DF-CEBC, with appropriate modifications of focus.
2 This would include any emotional problem(s) they have about their practical problem(s).
3 Cavanagh (2005) argues that these are i) when the emotional problem is of recent origin or occurs intermittently; ii) the responses of your coachee to the adversity are distressing to the person, but lie within a mild to moderate range of distress; iii) your coachee's emotional problem is limited to a certain situation or aspect of the person's life; iv) the person is not defensive with respect to the problem; and v) the person is open to address and change the problem.

Chapter 5

A framework to guide and implement cognitive-emotive-behavioural coaching for practical problems (PPF-CEBC)

Problem-focused cognitive-emotive-behavioural coaching (PF-CEBC), as the name makes clear, is coaching that is focused on helping coachees to deal with their problems. As discussed in Chapter 3, such problems are either practical problems or emotional problems. A practical problem is one where your coachee is confused, tangled up with an issue or issues and needs clarity and order, which they hope to get by talking things through with someone, but they are not emotionally disturbed about the issue(s). An emotional problem is one where the person has an emotionally disturbed reaction to an adversity. Also, your coachee may have an emotional problem about their practical problem (for example, your coachee is confused about how to prioritise their workload (practical problem) and feels ashamed about their confusion (emotional problem)). In most cases, where your coachee has both types of problems about one issue, it is important to help them deal with their emotional problem first before helping them to address their practical problem. The reason for this is that dealing with a practical problem depends on your coachee being in a clear, problem-solving state of mind and having an emotional problem frequently interferes with such a mindset.

Having made the point that your coachee may have both a practical problem and an emotional problem about that practical problem, in this chapter I will deal with a framework that guides CEB coaching for practical problems (PPF-CEBC), and in Chapter 7, I will deal with a framework that guides CEB coaching for emotional problems (EPF-CEBC).

5.1. A problem-solving framework for guiding and implementing CEB coaching for practical problems

When a person seeks coaching for help with a practical problem – defined above as one "where your coachee is confused, tangled up with an issue or issues and needs clarity and order, which they hope to get by talking things through with someone, but they are not emotionally disturbed about the issue(s)" – your basic task is to help them order their thoughts and define the

Table 5.1 The PRACTICE problem-solving framework (adapted from Palmer, 2008)

	Thinking steps	Examples of problem-solving thinking
P	**P**roblem identification	• What is the problem or issue that I need to focus on?
R	**R**ealistic, relevant goal development	• What are the goals or objectives that I can realistically work towards, ones that will make a real difference for me?
A	**A**lternative potential solutions generated	• What have I tried already that has not worked? • Were there any elements of what I tried that were helpful on which I can build? • What are the possible ways that I can solve the problem or reach my goal or objective?
C	**C**onsideration of potential solutions	• What do I think of each of the potential solutions (e.g. what are their consequences?; are they consistent with my values?; what other aspects of each possible solution do I have to consider?)
T	**T**arget most feasible potential solution	• Having looked at each potential solution and its consequences, which one is likely to be the most feasible one that I can select?
I	**I**mplementation of chosen potential solution	• How am I going to best implement the chosen potential solution?
C	**C**onsolidation of the chosen potential solution	• How am I going to ensure that I have given the chosen potential solution the best chance to see if it yields the results I want?
E	**E**valuation	• How successful was the potential solution? If successful, it becomes the solution. • If not, I need to try another potential solution until I find one that works.

problem in terms that are solvable. Then, you can help them by using one of the many problem-solving frameworks that exist in the helping literature.

5.1.2. The PRACTICE model of problem-solving

The framework that I use and will present here is one that has been designed specifically for use in coaching rather than counselling and/psychotherapy. It is known as PRACTICE and was designed by the British coaching psychologist Stephen Palmer (2008). Let me discuss each of the eight steps of the model, which is presented in Table 5.1.

5.1.2.1. Step 1: Problem identification

If your coachee has come to coaching for help with one specific practical problem, then problem identification is a straightforward matter. More frequently, however, when your coachee comes for help with practical problems it is because they are overwhelmed and "can't see the woods for the trees". When this happens, your basic task is to respond to your coachee in a way that brings structure to their experience. This will help them to identify the problems that they want help with and to prioritise them in the order that they wish to deal with them. In PPF-CEBC, you encourage your coachee to focus on one problem at a time and the selected problem in this context is known as the target problem.

5.1.2.2. Realistic, relevant goal development

Once you have helped your coachee to identify their target problem, it is important to help them to set goal. CEB coaches often use the acronym SMART to help their coachee to set goals; this stands for: specific; measurable; achievable; relevant; time-bound. Thus, you should wherever practicable and with your coachee's agreement help them to set goals that are:

5.1.2.2.1. SPECIFIC

This makes it clear what outcome your coachee is working towards so that you, your coachee and any stakeholders know that the goal has been achieved.

5.1.2.2.2. MEASURABLE

Encourage your coachee to devise a way of measuring their progress towards their goal and also when it has been achieved.

5.1.2.2.3. ACHIEVABLE

By an achievable goal, I mean two things here. First, a goal that is achievable is one that is within the power of your coachee to achieve. Thus, "My goal is for my team to hit their monthly target" is not within the direct control of your coachee because that depends, ultimately, on the behaviour of the people in your coachee's team. "My goal is to give daily feedback to my team to give them the best chance of hitting their monthly target" is with the control of your coachee since it depends on their behaviour and is therefore achievable. Second, a goal that is achievable is realistic given the resources that your coachee has at their disposal.

5.1.2.2.4. RELEVANT

A relevant goal is one that, if achieved, will make a real difference to your coachee given where they currently are in their life.

5.1.2.2.5. TIME-BOUND

It is important to determine with your coachee how much time they have to achieve their goal since the amount of time at your coachee's disposal will have a significant influence on the goal that they choose. It is also important to help your coachee to agree with themself when they are going to do goal-related tasks. Thus, a coachee who is going to devote a large chunk of time to regular goal-directed activity can afford to be more ambitious in goal-setting than the coachee who is only going to devote a small chunk of time to infrequent goal-directed activity.

I have already mentioned that I see CEBC as a fusion of what you bring to the process as coach and what your coachee brings to the process. You are bringing your expertise as a CEB coach and in this context an aspect of your expertise is the SMART approach to goal-setting. However, your coachee may have other ideas about goal setting and it is important that you refer this to the reflection process so that you can arrive at a shared approach to goal-setting.

5.1.2.3. *A*lternative potential solutions generated

You and your coachee now know what the problem is that they are facing and you have agreed on what would constitute a goal with respect to that problem. Before moving on to the next step, which is to help your coachee to generate a number of alternative solutions to the problem, it is useful to discover what they have already tried to solve the problem.

5.1.2.3.1. ASSESS PREVIOUS PROBLEM-SOLVING ATTEMPTS

It is very likely that what your coachee has already tried to do to solve the problem has not proven effective, after all they have come to you for coaching help to solve the problem. However, it is important that you know what the previous attempts are so that you don't end up by encouraging your coachee to do something that they have already tried that has proven not to work. Also, there may be certain elements of what they have tried that were useful and it is important to know about these so that you can build on these elements rather than starting from scratch.

5.1.2.3.2. INITIATE BRAINSTORMING

Brainstorming is a useful strategy designed to encourage your client to be creative in their thinking, free from the concern that they have come up with something silly or stupid, for example. Indeed, as coach you might join in this process by modelling the free and unconstrained thinking that you are trying to encourage in your coachee. It sometimes happens that the brainstorming yields an effective potential solution to the coachee's problem that they would not have thought of otherwise.

5.1.2.4. Consideration of potential solutions

Once your coachee has completed the process of generating potential solutions, it is time for them to consider and evaluate each one. Normally, at this point, the sole emphasis is on the likely consequences of implementing each possible solution (Palmer, 2008). This, of course, is an important consideration because, after all, your coachee has come to you for help with solving their problem(s). When considering the consequences of potential solutions, you not only need to help your coachee think of the effectiveness of each possible solution with respect to its problem-solving potential, you also need to help them to think of other consequences as well (e.g. the impact of the potential solution on others involved in that area of your coachee's life; and the longer-term effects of solving the problem using the approach selected to do so).

However, there are other issues for your coachee to take into account when considering whether or not to implement each of their generated potential solutions. One such important consideration concerns the relationship between a potential solution and the coachee's *values*. Thus, from a pragmatic perspective your coachee may have generated a potential solution with the best chance of solving their problem, but implementing it might compromise one or more of their values and therefore they might hold back from selecting this potential solution as one to try out.

Another issue concerns whether or not your coachee has the necessary capability, in the first place, or the necessary skills, in the second place, to carry out a potential solution which they consider to have the best chance of solving their problem if implemented. As I discussed in Chapter 3, if your coachee does not have the capability to implement a potential solution then the matter is clear, the coachee won't be able to implement it. However, if they don't have the skills (but they do have the capability) to do so, then you will need to discuss with them whether it is worth it for them to learn the requisite skills in order to implement the chosen potential solution. The more plausible and potentially effective solutions are available to your coachee, the less likely it is that they will choose to learn the aforementioned skills. However, if the chosen potential solution is the only feasible solution then they probably will choose to learn the skills to implement it.

5.1.2.5. Target the most feasible potential solution

At the end of the consideration process described above, your coachee should, ideally, be in a position to select one or sometimes more potential solutions that they hope will actually solve their problem. If more than one solution is chosen, have your coachee rank them in the order that they will use them. The first on the list is known as the target solution. If this turns out not to be effective, then encourage your coachee to select the next one on the list and so on.

5.1.2.6. Implementation of the chosen potential solution

Once your coachee has selected a target potential solution, they need help with implementing it. A number of issues need to be considered jointly with your coachee when discussing the implementation of their target potential solution. These include:

- Breaking the chosen potential solution into manageable steps
- Deciding when to take these steps, where and with whom
- Identifying potential obstacles to the implementation of the potential solution and dealing with these obstacles.

5.1.2.7. Consolidation of the chosen potential solution

It is quite rare for a coachee to solve their problem the first time they implement their chosen potential solution and therefore some thought has to be given to the following question: "How am I going to ensure that I have given the chosen potential solution the best chance to see if it yields the results I want?" The answer to this question will ensure that your coachee has utilised the actual potency of their target potential solution to effect the change that they seek.

During this process, you will discuss with your coachee their experiences of implementing their chosen potential solution. This will enable your coachee to make any modifications to the potential solution that they are carrying out and how they are executing it. It also gives you both the opportunity to identify and discuss any actual obstacles your coachee encountered during this phase of PPF-CEBC.

5.1.2.8. Evaluation

When your coachee has implemented the chosen potential solution over the selected consolidation time period you can then help them to evaluate its effects. Has it actually solved the problem? If not, does it look like it has the potential to solve the problem given more implementation time? If so, then encourage your coachee to carry on with the chosen problem-solving tasks. If not, encourage them to select the next potential solution on their list and use the same steps as above. Work in this way until the problem has been solved. If it is still not solved, it may be that your coachee has an emotional problem about the practical problem that needs addressing.

5.2. Drawing on your clients' experiences, strengths and resources for solving practical problems

As I have already noted, this book outlines a cognitive-emotive-behavioural approach to coaching. In doing so it aims to be flexible and pluralistic in viewpoint. As such, CEB coaches are not just interested in offering their coachees a framework for understanding and dealing with their practical problems (as defined here). They are also interested in encouraging their coachees to apply their own experiences, strengths and resources for solving past practical problems to solving their present one.

5.2.1. Helping your coachee to discover and apply their past success experiences at solving practical problems

Frameworks like PRACTICE offer your coachee a systematic approach to practical problem-solving that may be in tune with their own natural approach to dealing with practical problems or may be very foreign to the person. When it is tune with the person's natural style it can offer the person an opportunity to fill in any gaps in their problem-solving style that may make a difference to them solving their target problem.

When the PRACTICE framework, for example, is very foreign to your coachee, then two things may happen. First, they may see its value and wish to learn it and apply it to solve their problem even though it goes against their natural problem-solving grain. In which case your task is to teach them how to use it while recognising the difficulty they will experience in learning it and applying it.

Second, they may be resistant to it and, if so, there is little to be gained for you to attempt to win them over. In this case, you need to find out what past successes they have had in solving similar practical problems. In doing so, you need to ask them to come up with specific examples of these past successes and then your task is to interview them closely to discover what was effective about what they did and what was ineffective. Then you take what was effective and work with your coachee to discover how they can apply this to solving their current target problem.

Finally, even if you teach your coachee the PRACTICE framework, there is still much value to be derived by discovering their past effective problem-solving strategies in order to help them incorporate their own successful strategies into the PRACTICE framework.

5.2.2. Helping your coachee to identify and apply their strengths to the practical problem-solving process

Coaching was originally devised as a process that helps people get more out of themselves, their relationships and their lives in general. In this book,

I discuss this traditional approach to coaching in Chapters 9 and 10. However, in practice cognitive-behavioural coaches found that people sought help not just to develop themselves, but also to solve a host of practical and emotional problems. One of the hallmarks of CEB coaching in this latter area is that it applies important principles from development-focused coaching to problem-focused coaching. An example of this is the emphasis placed on discovering your coachee's general strengths as a person and encouraging them to apply these to the solving of their target practical problem. In this context, strengths are the internal attributes or personality traits and characteristics that can help your coachee to solve their practical problem(s). To this end, here are some sample questions you can ask your coachee about their strengths:

- "What would you say are your strengths as a person that you can bring to the coaching process to help solve your target problem?"
- "What would others who know you well say were your strengths as a person that you can bring to the coaching process to help solve your target problem?"
- "If you were being interviewed for a job that involved solving the practical problems of others that are like your target problem, and you were asked what strengths you had as a person that you would bring to helping these others, how would you respond?"

In addition, you can use a variety of questions that are used by graduate recruiters in what are known as "strengths-based interviews". Please note that you may have to search a little for your coachee's strengths in the responses to such questions. Then you will need to help the person think about how they would apply their answers to solving their target practical problem.

- What are you good at?
- What do you enjoy doing in your spare time?
- Tell me about something you are particularly proud of.
- What do you do first on your to-do list?
- When would your friends and family say that you are at your happiest?
- What tasks or activities come easily to you?
- Describe a situation in which you feel most like yourself.

Some coaches like to get the above information about their coachee's strengths before they take their coachee through a structured approach to practical problem-solving such as PRACTICE (discussed above). They do this so that they and/or their coachee can feed in this information where appropriate. Other coaches prefer to ask about their coachee's strengths when there is a suitable place to do so during the process. My own approach is to outline these two different approaches so that my coachee can express their opinion about what may be most helpful to them. I will generally go along with their views unless

I have a strong reason not to, and in this case I will disclose the reason and refer the issue to the reflection process for discussion and resolution.

5.2.3. Helping your coachee to identify and use their resources in the practical problem-solving process

If strengths are "the internal attributes or personality traits and characteristics that can help your coachee to solve their practical problem(s)" (see above), resources are the practical tools or people present in your coachee's life that are available to assist in problem-solving. The example I often keep in mind when distinguishing between a strength and a resource is this. If you want to hire someone to help you move house, you will look for someone who is dependable (strength) and who has a reliable car (resource). One without the other will be less effective than both together. In this section, you are looking for the resources that will help your coachee to use their strengths to best effect in solving their target practical problem.

Here are some sample questions you can ask your coachee about their resources:

- What resources do you have access to that could help you solve your practical problem? If you don't have access to these resources, is there anybody who can help you get access to them?
- Which people do you have access to who may help you solve your practical problem? Who are they and what can each of them bring to the situation that may be helpful to you in solving your practical problem?
- What information do you need that will help you solve your practical problem? Where can you get this information?
- What resources in the community might be helpful to you in solving the practical problem?

As discussed above with respect to your coachee's strengths, there are three approaches to obtaining information about resources that may help your coach solve their practical problem: i) before taking them though a structured approach to problem-solving like PRACTICE; ii) while doing so; or iii) coachee choice concerning the best way for them.

In the following chapter, I will present a case showing PPF-CEBC in action which will demonstrate how the issues presented in this chapter can be implemented within the context of an actual coaching relationship.

Chapter 6

Lionel: an example of practical problem-focused cognitive-emotive-behavioural coaching (PPF-CEBC)

In this chapter, I will discuss the case of Lionel, a 33-year-old manager. Lionel was married with two children and worked for an investment bank. Lionel was struggling a little at work and his own line manager recommended that he see one of the company's internal coaches, but Lionel was uncomfortable with this idea, preferring to see a coach outside the company. It was decided, therefore, that his company would fund three months' coaching with an external coach of Lionel's choice.

6.1. Greeting Lionel

Lionel wanted specifically to see a cognitive-behavioural coach because his friend had had cognitive-behavioural therapy and from what he said Lionel liked some of the ideas and thought that they could be helpful to him. After some research, Lionel found Simon, a CEB coach who he contacted on the number on Simon's website.

Simon returned Lionel's call and suggested that they had a brief 10-minute telephone or Skype call to see if Simon could help Lionel and, if not, suggest someone who might help him. Lionel agreed and they set up a 10-minute telephone screening conversation.

6.2. The brief real-time initial screening conversation with Lionel

If you recall, the major purposes of what I called, in Chapter 4, a "brief, real-time conversation" was for you i) to rule out the possibility of taking on the person for coaching[1] and ii) to set up a face-to-face assessment-based session if it turned out that you might be able to help the person.

6.2.1. "What are you looking for?"

In response to Simon's question, Lionel said that he was struggling at work and had a lot of work to do and people to manage. He said that he had no real system to employ to help him organise his work so that he felt he was fire-fighting rather than being on top of things. He said he wanted help in getting organised. Lionel did not mention any disturbed emotional responses to this situation. This appeared indicative of a practical problem where a person "is confused, tangled up with an issue or issues and needs clarity and order, which they hope to get by talking things through with someone, but they are not emotionally disturbed about the issue(s)".

6.2.2. "Who suggested that you contact me and why?"

Lionel mentioned that he wanted a cognitive-behavioural coaching because his friend had CBT and Lionel liked the structure and practical nature of a cognitive-behavioural approach. Lionel mentioned that he found Simon from an internet search and liked his website and the fact that Simon was slightly older than him.

6.2.3. "Are you looking for ongoing coaching or a time-limited contract? If the latter, how much time or how many sessions were you thinking of?"

Lionel said that his company would fund three months' of coaching.

6.2.4. "Who will be funding your coaching?"

As mentioned above, Lionel's company would be funding his coaching and Simon asked Lionel to find out what his sponsor's expectations were with respect to any involvement in his coaching before they made any contract to work with one another.

6.2.5. "My fee is £... per session. Is this acceptable to you or the person funding your coaching?"

Lionel said that Simon's fee was within the budget he was given for coaching by his company.

6.2.6. "Is there anything important you would like to tell me at this stage?"

Lionel wanted to know about Simon's confidentiality policy and was reassured by his answer.

6.2.7. Decision time

From what Lionel had told him, Simon thought that he could help him and they decided to meet for a face-to-face session for an hour to carry out a fuller assessment, discuss the practicalities of coaching and deal with any of Lionel's queries before going on to the contracting phase, if appropriate.

6.3. The face-to-face assessment-based session

As Lionel elaborated on his problem with Simon, it became clearer that his problem was practical rather than emotional in nature. He lacked any clear method of prioritising his work and his managerial responsibilities, which resulted in him feeling out of control and at the mercy of events and people in his work place. His goal, in relation to this problem, was to find such a method that would lead him to have that sense of control that he lacked. At the end of this conversation, Simon thought that Lionel would be a good candidate for practical problem-focused CEBC.

6.4. Contracting with Lionel

Having decided that he could help Lionel, Simon moved into the contracting phase of the session. Let's pick up on the dialogue at this point.

SIMON: Based on what you have said so far, Lionel, I think you are a good candidate for what we call "practical problem-focused cognitive-behavioural coaching".[2] This type of coaching is primarily for a person who is really caught with an issue and needs to talk things over with someone to gain clarity and see a way forward. It is designed to help the person replace a sense of chaos with a sense of order. Although the person may well be confused, they are not emotionally disturbed about the issue. How does that sound?
LIONEL: It sounds just what I am looking for.
SIMON: Great. So, shall we see if we can get on the right track on a number of issues and then, if we can, develop a contract to work with one another?
LIONEL: Sounds like a plan.
SIMON: OK, so, I will now go over a number of areas and then, after we have agreed verbally, I will have the contract typed up and we can both sign it. OK?
LIONEL: Fine.
SIMON: OK, so you mentioned that your company were going to fund your coaching for three months. What's your view on the best way we could use the time in organising sessions?
LIONEL: Once a week would suit me.
SIMON: OK, we can revisit that later if we need to. So, shall I set the start of the contract for next week, with our last session three months from next week's date?
LIONEL: That's fine.
SIMON: You also mentioned that my fee was in budget. Did they mention how they would pay the fee?

LIONEL: Oh, you can invoice me and I will pay you and they will reimburse me when I give them the receipts. Is that OK?
SIMON: That's fine. On that point I have a 48-hour cancellation policy where I will invoice you if you don't me give me 48 hours' notice, unless there is a serious medical emergency for you or anyone in your immediate family. Also, if I don't give you 48 hours' notice if I cancel a session then you get the next session free unless I or one of my immediate family have a medical emergency. Is that OK?
LIONEL: That's clear and fair. So, if my company call me to an urgent meeting I still have to pay?
SIMON: Yes. Now some coaches and coachees agree at the outset that they will have some planned contact between sessions which is invoiced for. What is your view on that issue?
LIONEL: I don't think that will be relevant.
SIMON: OK, we can revisit the issue if it becomes relevant. Now let's move on to confidentiality. I went over this when we spoke briefly on the phone, but let me reiterate what I said. My standard practice here is to keep everything confidential with the following exceptions: a) if you pose a risk to your own life and well-being and are not prepared to take steps to protect yourself; b) if you pose a risk to the life or well-being of others and are not prepared to take steps to protect them; c) if you disclose information that I am mandated to disclose to the authorities, such as child abuse; d) if I am legally mandated to disclose my notes; and e) if my fees are not met after I have taken reasonable steps to recover them. Do you agree to this?
LIONEL: Yes, that is fine.
SIMON: So, that just leaves the issue of confidentiality and your company. I asked you to check out with them what their involvement would be in your coaching. What did they say?
LIONEL: Well, I spoke to HR and my line manager and they both said the same thing. They were happy to fund the coaching sessions, but they don't need any reports or anything. They also said that if you want to discuss anything with them that would be fine.
SIMON: I would only do that if we both agreed that it would be useful and, if so, I would need your written permission to make such contact.
LIONEL: That's fine.
SIMON: Let's talk about our respective roles and responsibilities. Let's start with our respective roles. I see my role as coach to listen attentively to what you say, to offer you a framework to understand your problem, to help you set a goal with respect to that problem and to offer you a pathway to achieving your goal. I see your role as coachee to tell me about the problem for which you are seeking help as honestly as you can, to give me feedback on the frameworks I offer you about the problem and how it can be addressed, to set a goal with respect to the problem and to give me

your own ideas about the problem and how it can be best addressed. We will then discuss our respective views and come up with a jointly agreed framework for understanding and dealing with the problem. What's your view on our roles?

LIONEL: So, we will be working together as a team and you will be expecting my input on everything. Is that right?

SIMON: That's well put. Is that agreeable?

LIONEL: That's what I was hoping for.

SIMON: Great. Now let me say something about how I see our respective responsibilities. Let me begin with my own. I am responsible for bringing my expertise as a coach to the process and for communicating my ideas as clearly as possible. I am responsible for making suggestions at various points based on my expertise, for helping you to put any jointly agreed activities into practice and for helping you to monitor your progress towards your goals. It is also my responsibility to help you to identify and deal with any obstacles along the pathway to your goal and to help you to voice any doubts, reservations and objections you may have to any aspect of coaching. It is my responsibility then to initiate a discussion of these doubts etc., so that we can deal with them. How does that sound?

LIONEL: That's fine. I have read that some coaches send their coachees reminders to do their homework tasks and ask for daily progress reports from coachees. Do you do that?

SIMON: As a general rule, no. I see reminding yourself to do any homework tasks as one of your responsibilities and I expect you to keep daily records of progress, if we agree that it is appropriate for you to do so, and let me know of this progress at every weekly session. Having said that, if we both agree to such reminders and to daily progress reports then we would incorporate these into our coaching, but it would not be my first line of approach. Does that answer your question?

LIONEL: Yes.

SIMON: So, I have mentioned one of your responsibilities in coaching – to remind yourself to carry out mutually agreed homework tasks. Let me mention others. My view is that you can't do my work for me and I can't do your work for you. So, your work is to put into practice anything that we have agreed that you will do between sessions and to disclose any obstacles that you encounter to doing that. It is your responsibility to keep records of your progress so that we can both monitor this progress in coaching sessions. It is also your responsibility to tell me about any doubts, reservations or objections you have to any aspect of the coaching process so we can discuss and deal with them. How does all that sound?

LIONEL: Perfectly reasonable and acceptable.

SIMON: Now let me tell you about my referral policy. If it transpires during coaching that you require help beyond my skills or expertise, I am duty bound to suggest that you seek such help elsewhere and will make a judicious referral where possible. All this will be done in discussion with you. Are you agreeable?

LIONEL: Yes. Do you think that might happen?

SIMON: I have no way of knowing at the moment. So, that covers all the items I want to discuss. Do you have any items you would like to form part of our contract?

LIONEL: Not that I can think of at the moment.

SIMON: OK, so let me suggest this. I will have the contract typed up and sent to you before we meet next week. If you are happy with it then sign it and bring it next week. If there are any changes that you want to make or any additions you want to suggest we can discuss them at the beginning of the session. OK?

LIONEL: OK.

6.5. Problem identification

At the first coaching session, Lionel revealed that he was happy to sign the contract that Simon sent after the assessment and contracting session, but suggested a few minor changes in wording first. Then, after they both signed the contract, Simon suggested it would be helpful for both of them to get a clear understanding of the problem for which Lionel was seeking help.

SIMON: So, Lionel, you mentioned at our first meeting that you were struggling at work. You have a lot of work on and a lot of people to manage and you don't feel on top of things. Is that right?

LIONEL: Yes.

SIMON: So, what contributes most to you not being on top of things, your own workload or managing others?

LIONEL: Mainly managing others.

SIMON: Can you tell me more about that?

LIONEL: Well, I manage about ten people and they are quite demanding. They come to me quite a lot with their problems and want to talk to me there and then.

SIMON: And how do you respond?

LIONEL: Well, I leave my own work and help them.

SIMON: Ok, so how much time does that take?

LIONEL: Well it can vary, but it can be anything from 5 minutes to 30 minutes.

SIMON: And how many times does that happen a day?

LIONEL: Oh anywhere from three times to ten times.

[As is typical of a CEB coach, Simon is asking Lionel a lot of questions to get a lot of data.]

SIMON: And do you go back to your own work straightaway?

LIONEL: Well, I try to, but it's difficult.

SIMON: Turning to your own work, aside from the interruptions, what is problematic about it for you?

LIONEL: I find it difficult to prioritise my work, so I end up doing whatever is next in my in-tray.

6.6. Realistic, relevant goal development

In coaching for practical problems, it is important to help your coachee have a clear idea of what solution they are aiming for. This is the goal-setting part of the PRACTICE model discussed fully in Chapter 5.

SIMON: So now we are clear on what the problem is, what do you see as the solution to the problem?
LIONEL: Well, I guess I would like to feel on top of things at work.
SIMON: On a 1–10 scale where "1" represents "not feeling on top of things at all at work" and "10" represents "feeling completely on top of things at work", where would you rate yourself at the moment?
LIONEL: About a "2".
SIMON: And what would you have to do to feel on top of things at work?
[This is a typical CEBC question. In Chapter 5, I discussed the SMART approach to goal-setting and what Simon is doing here is encouraging Lionel to give the specific referents to his broader feeling-based goal.]
LIONEL: Well, let me see … I guess I need to come to an agreement with the people I manage concerning when they can ask for help.
SIMON: So, if I helped you to find an agreement that worked in practice and led you to feel that you were on top of things at work, then that would be one of your goals?
LIONEL: Yes, it would.
SIMON: What about your own work? What would you have to do to feel on top of your own workload?
LIONEL: I guess I would have to find a way of prioritising my work so that I was responding to real need rather than doing what was on top of my in-tray.
SIMON: So, if I helped you to find an arrangement which worked with the people you manage so that you felt on top of your manager's role and if I helped you to find a system that helped you to prioritise your own workload so that you felt on top of it, would that solve your problem?
LIONEL: If both of those worked then yes.
[Note that Simon has not asked Lionel to be more specific about the arrangement and system mentioned. This is because the work he is going to do with Lionel on these issues will lead to this clarity and can't be specified in advance.]

6.7. Helping your coachee to identify and use their strengths and resources in the practical problem-solving process

In Chapter 5, I discussed the importance of encouraging your coachee to bring their strengths and resources to the problem-solving process. If you recall, strengths are the internal attributes or personality traits and characteristics that can help your coachee to solve their practical problem(s), while resources are the practical tools or people present in your coachee's life that are available to assist in problem-solving.

After discussing these two points, Lionel thought that the strength that would serve him best in helping him to solve his problem was persistence, and the resource that he could call on which would be most useful was his friend Christopher, who was very good at solving problems.

6.8. Alternative potential solutions generated

The next stage in the problem-solving process known as PRACTICE is helping your coachee to generate potential solutions to their problem that they have not already tried. This initially involves a period of brainstorming. But first, you need to discover what your coachee has already tried to solve the problem so that you don't encourage them to use ineffective solution attempts.

6.8.1. Lionel's previous problem-solving attempts

Lionel's previous attempts to solve both his management problem and his workload problem had ultimately proven unsuccessful. With the workload issue, Lionel had tried to put his work into three piles of priority: high, medium and low. While this had initially proved useful, Lionel was not able to maintain it when others asked him to change his prioritising. This gave Simon the opportunity to refine their joint understanding of Lionel's workload problem.

SIMON: So initially your method of prioritising your work by putting it into three piles worked until other people effectively challenged it. Is that right?
LIONEL: Yes.
SIMON: What would have happened if you had explained to people that you would do a piece of work and had given them a time when it would have been done consistent with your priority system?
LIONEL: They would have understood that.
SIMON: So, it's not a case of them giving you some kind of negative response?
LIONEL: No, it's just that I don't like saying no to people.
SIMON: So, if you could say "no" to people, would that make a difference?
LIONEL: A big difference.
SIMON: In what way?
LIONEL: It would mean that I could work to my own system rather than putting their needs first.
SIMON: Do you think that this is a factor in your problem with managing others?
LIONEL: Yes, I do.

[While it may not seem that Simon is following the PRACTICE structure, he is doing so flexibly. It is only in reviewing Lionel's past attempts at solving his problems that Simon is able to clarify the true nature of his problem. He does not say no to people when it would be in his interests to do so. This is a potential obstacle that Simon needs to help Lionel with before implementing his chosen potential solution(s).]

6.8.2. Initiate brainstorming

After clarifying Lionel's problem, Simon suggested that they brainstorm possible solutions to the problem as manifest in Lionel managing his own workload and managing others. These were as follows:

6.8.2.1. Managing own workload

- Explain to people that I have a problem saying no and request that they don't put pressure on me
- Listen to what others want me to do and when they want me to do it, then tell them that I will think about it and let them know when I can finish the task, having assessed it using my ABC priority ranking system
- Involve HR in the solution of the problem
- Ignore what others want and just concentrate on my own work
- Spend more time at work so I can finish my workload without talking to others.

6.8.2.2. Managing other people

- Encourage people who I manage to use the ABC priority ranking system with their own work and to come to me for help only when they have exhausted their own attempts to solve their problem
- Develop an office hour system when the people I manage can come and see me
- Encourage people I manage to come to see me with potential solutions to problems not just problems
- Develop an appointment system with the people I manage so that a) they get used to waiting and b) they know that I am not immediately available to help them.

6.9. Consideration of potential solutions

Simon's next task was to help Lionel stand back and consider each of these potential solutions using a number of criteria.

Advantages of..

Short-term advantages

For myself:

1..
2..
3..
4..
5..

For others:

1..
2..
3..
4..
5..

Long-term advantages

For myself:

1..
2..
3..
4..
5..

For others:

1..
2..
3..
4..
5..

Disadvantages of ....

Short-term disadvantages

For myself:

1..
2..
3..
4..
5..

For others:

1..
2..
3..
4..
5..

Long-term disadvantages

For myself:

1..
2..
3..
4..
5..

For others:

1..
2..
3..
4..
5..

Figure 6.1 Cost–benefit analysis form

6.9.1. The pragmatic criterion

The main criterion in problem-solving is a pragmatic one: which solution is best going to solve Lionel's problem? To this end, Simon encouraged Lionel to complete a cost–benefit analysis, as shown in Figure 6.1.

As this form shows, Lionel is asked to consider the advantages and disadvantages of each potential solution, from a short-term and long-term perspective as these affect Lionel and other people deemed affected by this issue. In Lionel's case, these other people are a) those who give him work to do and b) those he manages at work.

6.9.2. The values criterion

The values criterion asks Lionel to consider each potential solution from the perspective of values. Is each potential solution consistent with his values? Does any potential solution violate any of his values?

6.9.3. The capability criterion

The capability criterion asks Lionel to consider whether he has the capability to carry out each of the potential solutions. If he judges that he lacks the capability to carry out a particular potential solution, this automatically rules it out.

6.9.4. The skills criterion

The skills criterion asks Lionel to consider whether he has the skills to carry out each of the potential solutions. If he judges that he lacks the skills to carry out a particular potential solution, then Simon will help him to acquire those skills if the solution is otherwise the best available, or refer him to someone who can help him do so.

As a homework assignment, Lionel thought that it was a good idea to discuss these potential solutions with his friend Christopher, who he nominated earlier as a person/resource who was a good problem-solver.

6.10. Target the most feasible potential solution

At this point, Lionel and Simon have amassed a large amount of data which they then discussed fully, informed also by the views of Christopher, Lionel's friend. Based on these discussions, Lionel decided to target the following as the most feasible potential solutions:

- *Problem with workload*: Listen to what others want me to do and when they want me to do it. Then tell them that I will think about it and let

them know when I can finish the task, having assessed it using my ABC priority ranking system.
- *Problem with managing others*: Encourage people who I manage to use the ABC priority ranking system with their own work and to come to me for help only when they have exhausted their own attempts to solve their problem, and develop an appointment system with those people so that a) they get used to waiting and b) they learn that I am not immediately available to help them.

You will note that the most feasible potential solution to Lionel's problem with managing others is a combination of two potential solutions developed in the brainstorming phase.

6.11. Implementation of the chosen potential solutions

In order to implement Lionel's target solutions, both he and Simon decided that they first needed to deal with the issue that they both identified earlier as a potential obstacle to Lionel solving his problems: his difficulty saying no to people at work when they ask him to do something for them.

6.11.1. Dealing with Lionel's potential obstacle before implementation

SIMON: Before we talk about implementing the potential solutions that you have selected, we need to address your difficulty about saying "no" to people at work. Would now be a good time to do that?
LIONEL: Yes.
SIMON: You mentioned that your difficulty saying "no" was not connected with you predicting a negative response from people. What do you think it is connected with?
LIONEL: I'm not sure, but I just like being helpful to people.
SIMON: Is it possible for you to be helpful to people and say "no" to them?
[Here Simon is using a pluralistic concept of both/and.]
LIONEL: I guess so. I'm not quite sure what you mean?
SIMON: Well, if you say to someone at work who has asked you to do a task for them that you will do it by a certain time, but not immediately, are you saying "no" to them and still helping them?
LIONEL: Oh, I see what you mean. Yes.
SIMON: You have a young son. If he asks you to help him and you do so immediately, what are you teaching him?
LIONEL: Well, I am not teaching him patience.
SIMON: So, is it possible to help someone and say "no" to them?
LIONEL: Yes, it is.

SIMON: Let's apply this to your workload. If you do a task that someone gives you immediately, what are you teaching them?
LIONEL: That I will do any work I will give them immediately.
SIMON: And will that help you to feel on top of things at work?
LIONEL: No.
SIMON: And if you give them a time when you will do the task based on your priority assessment and they agree with that, are you helping them when you do the work on time?
LIONEL: Yes, I am.
SIMON: So, what can you conclude so far from this discussion?
LIONEL: That I can help myself by prioritising my workload and sticking to it and I can help others by promising them a time when I will do their work and I do it by that time.
SIMON: What do you think of this as a new guiding principle?
LIONEL: I like it.
SIMON: Do you think you could put it into practice?
LIONEL: Yes, I do.
SIMON: Do you have any doubts, reservations and objections to doing so?
LIONEL: Well, what if someone doesn't agree to wait?
SIMON: OK let's assume that. How could you respond?
LIONEL: Well, if it is my job to do it immediately, then I have to do so, but most of the time it isn't, so on those occasions I will explain the reasons for my priority assessment and that will probably do the trick. If they still don't agree, we can negotiate, but I am not going to do it immediately ... that's my plan anyway.
SIMON: OK, so let's now make an implementation plan to solve your workload problem.
[As Lionel and Simon focused on dealing with the potential obstacle in the context of his workload problem, it made sense for them to first work on this problem and then focus on Lionel's problem with managing people at work.]

6.11.2. Implementing the chosen potential solution to Lionel's problem with his workload

Simon and Lionel then drew up a plan to implement the selected solution to his problem with his workload. Broken down into its component parts the potential solution involved the following:

- Listen to what others want me to do and when they want me to do it
- Tell them that I will think about it and get back to them with a completion date
- Assess their task using my ABC priority ranking system
- Give them a completion date.

Based on these components, Lionel and Simon developed a grid on which Lionel collected data of work requests, his responses and what happened subsequently (see Table 6.1). The collection of such data is a hallmark of a problem-solving approach within PPF-CEBC.

6.11.3. Implementing the chosen potential solution to Lionel's problem with managing people at work

Simon and Lionel then drew up a plan to implement the selected solution to his problem with managing people at work. Broken down into its component parts the potential solution involved the following:

- Encourage people who I manage to use the ABC priority ranking system with their own work
- Encourage them to come to me for help only when they have exhausted their own attempts to solve their problem
- Develop an appointment system with those people so that a) they get used to waiting and b) they learn that I am not immediately available to help them.

Based on these components, Lionel and Simon developed another grid on which Lionel collected data of how he implemented each of these elements and what happened subsequently.

Because of the work that he had previously done with Simon on tolerating conflict better and not conceding to the viewpoint of the other at the first hint of conflict, Lionel was able to implement his chosen potential solution without much difficulty. Indeed, he was surprised with the response of those he managed at work, who welcomed what they saw as increased independence. It transpired that most of them thought that Lionel wanted them to go to him with their problems because he enjoyed helping them!

6.12. Consolidation of the chosen potential solution

Once Simon had helped Lionel to deal with his difficulty with conflict, he was able to maintain the gains that he made in dealing with his workload problem. He only once had to ask his line manager to intervene to resolve a disagreement with a colleague from another department about the completion date of a piece of work. Once it became clear to other work colleagues that he would not deal with their work requests immediately, Lionel received fewer requests of this nature.

Partly because the people he managed at work responded favourably to his new system for dealing with their work problems, Lionel was able to consolidate this potential solution quite easily.

Table 6.1 Lionel's data collection grid assessing his chosen potential solution to his problem with his workload

Date and time	Name of person	Listened to their request	1. Told them I would think about it and get back to them with a completion date 2. Person's response 3. My response (if relevant)	Assessed request using ABC priority system	1. Told them completion date 2. Person's response 3. My response (if relevant)	1. Completion date met (Y/N) 2. Person's response 3. My response (if relevant)	Evaluation of potential solution Using a 5 point scale (1-2-3-4-5) 1 = Did not solve problem 3 = Solved the problem in part 5 = Solved the problem in full	Comments

6.13. Evaluation

We have seen above that Lionel was able to implement his chosen solutions with his workload problem and management problem respectively. But what impact did these potential solutions have on Lionel's desire to be on top of things at work? At the end of the three-month contracted period of coaching, Lionel reported that on a 1–10 scale where "1" represented "not feeling on top of things at all at work" and "10" represented "feeling completely on top of things at work", his rating was "8", a score that he maintained at a follow-up session three months after coaching had ended. If you recall, before coaching started he rated himself "2" on the same scale. Lionel considered that he had solved both his work-related problems and was very pleased with Simon's coaching and its impact on him.

In the next chapter, I will discuss a framework to guide and implement CEB coaching when your coachee has an emotional problem. This is known as emotional problem-focused CEBC (EPF-CEBC).

Notes

1 If you are not the right professional to help the person, then refer the person to another professional (coaching or other professional), if you know of such an individual who could potentially help the person.
2 Although this book is on "cognitive-emotive-behavioural coaching", Simon uses the term "cognitive-behavioural coaching" with Lionel because the latter mentioned wanting a cognitive-behavioural approach to coaching.

Chapter 7

A framework to guide and implement cognitive-emotive-behavioural coaching for emotional problems (EPF-CEBC)

As outlined in Chapter 4, when your coachee seeks coaching help for an emotional problem, the person is experiencing an emotionally disturbed reaction to an adversity. While your coachee could have sought help from a therapist or counsellor for that problem, the fact that they have sought help from a coach may mean, as discussed earlier in the book, that seeking coaching is more acceptable to that person than seeking therapy or counselling. But what types of emotional problems are appropriate to be dealt with in coaching? Cavanagh (2005) suggests the following:

1. The emotional problem is of recent origin or occurs intermittently.
2. The responses of your coachee to the adversity are distressing to the person, but lie within a mild to moderate range of distress.
3. Your coachee's emotional problem is limited to a certain situation or aspect of the person's life.
4. The person is not defensive with respect to the problem.
5. The person is open to address and change the problem.

In addition to the situation where your coachee is primarily seeking coaching help for an emotional problem, there are two other situations where you may be called upon to help your coachee deal with problematic emotional and behavioural responses to an adversity. First, you may be called upon to deal with a situation where a coachee has an emotional problem about the practical problem for which they are primarily seeking help. It is best, in such circumstances, that you help your coachee get in the right frame of mind to deal with their practical problem and this involves helping them to address their emotional problem first.

Second, when you have a contract with your coachee for any type of CEBC, your coachee may experience obstacles along the way to achieving their development-based objectives or problem-based goals which may involve them having an emotionally disturbed reaction to what they encounter. If this happens you will be called upon to help them deal with their disturbed response.

There are a few frameworks that you can use in CEBC to guide you as you help your coachees to deal with emotional problems in coaching. I will outline the one that I tend to use; this is informed by the work of Albert Ellis and Aaron T. Beck, the two founding fathers of cognitive-behavioural therapy. However, as this book asks that you take a flexible and pluralistic approach to CEBC, this involves you being open to using other frameworks as well as to the ideas that your coachees have about understanding and dealing with their emotional problems and disturbed responses to practical problems and obstacles.

7.1. Understanding the Situational ABCDEFG framework

Briefly, the Situational ABCDEFG framework comprises eight components:

Situation – The situation or context in which the person's problem occurred
A = Adversity
B = Basic attitudes
C = Consequences of B
D = Dialectical engagement
E = Effects of D
F = Facilitating change
G = Goals

I will discuss the different components in the above order, although in coaching the order in which you may work with these components may vary.

7.1.1. Situation

It is very likely that your coachee's emotional problem occurs in a situational context even if this is held in their imagination. Certainly, the adversity with which your coachee has a problem does occur within such a context. It is useful to assume that it is possible to arrive at a description of this situation, particularly those aspects that are relevant to your coachee's problem.

Let's assume, for example, that your coachee has a problem with hurt feelings and describes a situation in which they felt this emotion. They tell you that they were walking along a road, passed by a colleague, greeted them, but received no response to their greeting. Your coachee tells you that they felt very hurt about their colleague ignoring them. Using the framework, it is important at this stage for you to distinguish the facts of the situation as described and the inference that your coachee made, which was their adversity (see the next section). These, then, are the facts of the matter as described by your coachee:

- "When walking along the road, I passed by a colleague."
- "I greeted the person as I walked by."
- "They did not say anything."

I will return to this example in the next section.

7.1.2. A = Adversity

People have emotional problems about life's adversities, which are negative events that have occurred in their life, that they think have occurred or that they predict will occur. Adversities tend to be inferences, which I discussed in Chapter 2. In helping your coachees to deal with their emotional problems, it is best if you help them to assume that their adversity-related inferences are correct even if they are distorted. Thus, in working with the coachee discussed above, it is important to say something like: "So you thought that your colleague ignored you. Let's assume for the moment that they did ..."

An alternative strategy is to help your coachee look at alternative inferences to explain their colleague's behaviour. Here are some examples:

- "My colleague did not see me."
- "My colleague did not hear what I was saying."
- "My colleague did not recognise me."
- "My colleague was preoccupied."
- "My colleague was too shy to say hello."

If you had taken this tack, it may have occurred to your coachee that any of the above inferences were more likely to have been true than the one they originally made and about which they felt very hurt. If they had accepted any of these inferences they would no longer experience hurt. However, they would not have gone on to deal with the adversity about which they originally disturbed themselves – being ignored by their colleague.

Thus, the Situational ABCDEFG framework that I am presenting here is one that holds that it is important to help people deal with adversities unless there is a good reason not to do so.

Common adversities that feature in coachees' emotional problems are rejection, criticism, failure, others acting badly and poor performance of self in public. I present a full list in Appendix 1.

7.1.3. B = Basic attitudes

The Situational ABCDEFG framework that I am presenting here holds that your coachees' basic attitudes are largely responsible for determining whether they respond to adversities in a disturbed manner or in a healthy manner. As I showed in Chapter 2, your coachee's disturbed responses (at C) to adversities (at A) are based on the rigid and extreme basic attitudes that they hold (at B) towards these adversities, while their healthy responses (at C) to the same adversities (at A) are based on the flexible and non-extreme basic attitudes that they hold (at B) towards A. In Table 2.2 in Chapter 2, I presented both sets of attitudes in full, and I will summarise these in Table 7.1.

Table 7.1 Summary of basic attitudes in the context of the ABC part of the Situational ABCDEFG framework

A = Adversity	

B = Rigid and extreme basic attitudes
Rigid attitude
Extreme attitudes
  - Awfulising attitude
  - Discomfort intolerance attitude
  - Depreciation attitude
	B = Flexible and non-extreme basic attitudes
	Flexible attitude
	Non-extreme attitudes
	  - Non-awfulising attitude
	  - Discomfort tolerance attitude
	  - Acceptance attitude

C = Disturbed responses (consequences of rigid and extreme basic attitudes) Emotional Behavioural Cognitive	C = Healthy responses (consequences of flexible and non-extreme basic attitudes) Emotional Behavioural Cognitive

7.1.4. C = Consequences of basic attitudes (B) towards adversity (A)

As noted in Table 7.1, "C" in the Situational ABCDEFG framework stands for the consequences of the basic attitudes (B) that your coachee holds towards adversity at A. As shown in that table, there are three types of consequences that as a coach you are interested in: your coachee's feelings, behaviour and thinking. When your coachee has an emotional problem about an adversity or a disturbed response to a practical problem or coaching-related obstacle, their emotions tend to be unhealthy, their behaviour tends to be unconstructive and their thinking tends to be highly distorted and skewed to the negative. When your coachee has dealt effectively with their emotional problem about the adversity or with their disturbed response to a practical problem or coaching-related obstacle, their emotions tend to be healthy, but still negative in tone,[1] their behaviour tends to be constructive and their thinking tends to be balanced and realistic. It follows from this that the goal of emotional problem-focused CEBC is to help your coachee deal healthily with the adversity in relation to this problem in the sense that as a result they will experience a healthy negative emotion, act constructively and think realistically in the face of this adversity. This is also the goal when your coachee is responding in a disturbed way to their practical problem or to any coaching-related obstacles that they might encounter.

7.1.4.1. Common emotional problems at "C"

While your coachee may frame their emotional problems for which they are seeking coaching help in different ways, when you consider these problems from the perspective of the emotions themselves, the following emotions are frequently encountered: anxiety, depression, unhealthy anger, guilt, shame, hurt, unhealthy jealousy and unhealthy envy. If you are to help coachees with these unhealthy negative emotions, you need to understand their dynamics and the dynamics of their healthy emotional alternatives. By "dynamics" here I mean the following:

- What these emotions (at C) are about (these are adversity-related inferences at A). These adversities are the same whether your coachee is experiencing an unhealthy negative emotion or a healthy negative emotion.
- On which set of attitudes these different emotions are based. Unhealthy negative emotions are based on rigid and extreme attitudes, while healthy negative emotions are based on flexible and non-extreme attitudes.
- What types of thinking and behaviour are associated with these different emotions.

I have presented the "dynamics" of the above eight unhealthy negative emotions with those of their healthy negative alternatives in Appendix 1. I recommend that you familiarise yourself with this material if you are going to help people with their emotional problems and with their disturbed responses to their practical problems and their coaching-related goals.

There is one important point that I wish to make about emotions. These are subjective experiences which your coachees will label in some way and these labels may not reflect the ones that you may use as a CEB coach. This is where the concepts of flexibility, pluralism and the coaching alliance become salient. Thus, although I have used a variety of emotion-related labels to distinguish between unhealthy negative emotions and their healthy negative emotional counterparts in Appendix 1, I encourage my coachees to use their own labels when making such distinctions. Once they have done so, I tend to make a note of this coachee-proposed terminology and use it going forward.

7.1.4.2. Behavioural responses at "C"

As you can see from the tables in Appendix 1, one of the ways that you can help yourself and your coachee decide whether they are responding healthily or unhealthily to an adversity, their practical problem or a coaching-related obstacle is to assess their behavioural responses to that adversity. As noted above, behaviours accompany your coachee's emotional response to an adversity and when they reflect what your coachee actually did in response to the adversity, practical problem or coaching-related obstacle, they are often more reliable indicators for the healthiness of your coachee's response when their report of their emotional experience is vague.

7.1.4.2.1. OVERT BEHAVIOUR VS. ACTION TENDENCY

As noted in Chapter 2, your coachee's overt behaviour is often based on a tendency or urge to act in a particular way. When you are trying to determine whether or not a coachee's anger response to a particular adversity, for example, is healthy or unhealthy and they reported that they took no action in the situation, discovering their action tendency can often help you to answer your question. Thus, if your coachee said in response to your question about their action tendency: "I felt like smashing him in the face, but didn't act on that," then this reveals a unhealthy response to the adversity, whereas if they said "I felt like asserting myself with him, but the context wasn't right," then this probably reveals a healthy adversity-related response.

7.1.4.2.2. BEHAVIOUR AS A WAY OF DEALING WITH THE PROBLEM

Not only can behaviour be seen as an expression of your coachee's emotional problem, for example, it can also be seen as a way of dealing with their associated disturbed feelings. Thus, when helping your coachee to understand their emotional problem, for example, find out if they use behaviour to avoid the problem, to withdraw quickly from the problem or even to over-compensate for their problem. Such behaviour is designed to help your coachee escape from the pain of the problem, but only serves unwittingly to maintain the problem. As such, it is important that you and your coachee both understand problem-maintaining behaviour and address it effectively during EPF-CEBC.

7.1.4.3. Thinking responses at "C"

As you can also see from the tables in Appendix 1, another way that you can help yourself and your coachee decide whether they are responding healthily or unhealthily to an adversity, their practical problem or a coaching-related obstacle is to assess their thinking subsequent to that adversity. Such thinking tends to be inferential in nature. As you can see from these tables, the inferences in the subsequent thinking at "C" that accompanies unhealthy negative emotions or UNEs (e.g. anxiety, depression, etc.) are much more negatively distorted than the inferences in the alternative thinking that accompanies healthy negative emotions or HNEs (e.g. concern, sadness etc.). These latter inferences tend to be more balanced and realistic than the former inferences. This difference also tends to be found in the respective images associated with UNEs and HNEs.

As with behaviour, thinking at "C" tends to be both an expression of your coachee's emotional problem and their way of dealing with the pain of the problem without addressing the problem. This is particularly seen in anxiety, where I distinguish between threat-exaggerated thinking (an expression of the problem) and safety-seeking thinking (an attempt to deal with emotional pain, but in ways that maintain it). You need to help your coachee deal with both types of subsequent thinking when helping them deal with their problem. I will discuss how to encourage your coachee to respond to such thinking later in the chapter and in Chapter 8.

7.1.5. D = Dialectical engagement

As I will discuss later in this chapter, it is important to help your coachee to understand the B–C connection. This involves them understanding the connection between their rigid and extreme basic attitudes towards the adversity (at A) in their emotional problem[2] and their disturbed responses to this adversity and b) their flexible and non-extreme basic attitudes towards A and their possible non-disturbed responses to this same A.

They may have also set these latter responses as their problem-related goal.[3] Therefore, you need to help them to stand back and examine these respective basic attitudes. Although this has traditionally been called "disputing", this term has negative connotations for many coaches as it suggests argumentation. After much consideration, I decided to use the term "dialectical engagement" for this process, which as you will notice begins with the letter "d" so that it fits in the ABCDEFG framework.

Using dialectical engagement with your coachee is a way of helping them to examine and query opposing attitudes to expose false, illogical and unhelpful ideas and find ideas that are truthful, sensible and helpful. This worked quite well, as rigid basic attitudes and flexible basic attitudes are opposing by nature, as are extreme basic attitudes and non-extreme basic attitudes.

The *goal* of engaging your coachee in the dialectical method is to help your coachee understand that their rigid and extreme basic attitudes are false, don't make sense and lead to poor results for the person and, by contrast, that their flexible and non-extreme basic attitudes are true, make sense and lead to good results for the person. If the process has been effective, then the effects will be experienced at point E in the framework.

I will discuss the practicalities of dialectical engagement later in the chapter.

7.1.6. E = Effects of dialectical engagement

The effects of using the dialectical engagement method are that your coachee understands intellectually that their rigid and extreme attitudes are false, illogical or don't make sense and have poor consequences for the person and that their flexible and non-extreme attitudes are true, logical or make sense and have good consequences for the person. Such intellectual understanding is an important, but insufficient, landmark in the change process. In order to experience real change your coachee needs the kind of understanding that has a decided impact on their feelings, behaviour and subsequent thinking. This is known as emotional understanding, as opposed to intellectual understanding. Such emotional understanding is achieved as a result of what I call the "facilitating change" part of the process (see below).

7.1.7. F = Facilitating change

Facilitating change involves your coachee working to strengthen their conviction in their flexible and non-extreme basic attitudes and to weaken their conviction in their rigid and extreme basic attitudes. This involves you both discussing how best to achieve this using a variety of cognitive, behavioural, emotive and imagery methods. It is particularly important for your coachee to think and act in ways that are consistent with their flexible and non-extreme attitudes and not to act and think in ways that unwittingly support the rigid and extreme attitudes that they are looking to change. The more this change process can be done within an emotional context, the more your coachee will strengthen their conviction in their flexible and non-extreme attitudes over the longer term.

7.1.8. G = Goals

As I discussed in Chapter 3, coaching is a purposive activity and your coachee has come to you for a purpose. In this chapter and the following one, I am discussing the situation where they come to you for coaching help for an emotional problem and they are looking to solve this problem in this way. It is a hallmark of the cognitive-emotive-behavioural approach to coaching that you help your coachee frame their problem-related goal as clearly as possible. Unlike the other seven steps of the Situational ABCDEFG framework, you can discuss your coachee's goals at any point in the coaching process. Thus, you can:

- Ask them what they want to achieve from coaching as soon as they sit down with you for the first time
- Ask them what they want to achieve with respect to the problem for which they are seeking help, but *before* you both understand it from a CEBC perspective
- Ask them what they want to achieve with respect to the problem for which they are seeking help, but *after* you both understand it from a CEBC perspective. In using the ABC part of the ABCDEFG framework (shown in Table 7.1), you will see that there are two C's – the C's on the left-hand side of the framework are related to the problem and those on the right-hand side could well be possible goals for your coachee to consider. I will exemplify this in the following chapter
- Stress the importance of goal-setting with respect to the adversity at A, if they try to bypass this in their goal-setting.

For example, if a person is anxious about interviews in case they dry up, but wants to improve their interviewee skills, then you need to help them to see that unless they address directly the adversity of drying up (which is always possible in an interview context), then any skills building that they engage in won't help them deal with the adversity. In this example, what the person is doing is attempting to redefine their problem as a practical one (of improving their interviewing skills) rather than deal with what they came in with: an emotional problem about drying up in interviews.

Once you and your coachee have carried out an assessment using the Situational ABC part of the Situational ABCDEFG framework, then, as I mentioned earlier, the C's that stem from the flexible and non-extreme basic attitudes on the right-hand side of Table 7.1 can serve as goals that drive the subsequent work that you both will do to address their emotional problem. These C's then become your coachee's goals at G in the framework. These goals at G then serve as beacons for your coachee to aim for, particularly when you are both working at stages D, E and F. Thus, when you are both engaged dialectically at D, examining both your coachee's rigid and extreme attitudes and their flexible and non-extreme attitudes, this engagement is driven by your coachee's goals at G. And once your coachee has opted to strengthen their flexible and non-extreme attitudes and weaken their rigid and non-extreme attitudes at E, the tasks your coachee carries out at F to facilitate meaningful change are also guided by their goals at G. Consequently, once your coachee has first set their goals at the assessment stage at C, it is important that you keep their goals to the fore at G during the change-based work that they will do at the D, E and F stages of the EPF-CEBC process.

7.2. Using the Situational ABCDEFG framework in EPF-CEBC

In the above section, I presented and discussed the Situational ABCDEFG framework as one that may guide your thinking about how to help coachees when they come for coaching help for their emotional problems (see Table 7.2 for a diagrammatic summary). In this section, I will discuss how to use the framework in actual EPF-CEB coaching. In the following chapter, I will show you how a CEB coach applied all this material in coaching work she did with one of her coachees who sought help for an emotional problem.

In Chapter 4, I discussed the very beginning phase of cognitive-emotive-behavioural coaching. One of the goals of that phase is for you and your coachee to agree on the type of coaching that is best for them: i) practical problem-focused coaching; ii) emotional problem-focused coaching; or iii) development-focused coaching. I will make the assumption in the rest of this chapter that your coachee has an emotional problem (or problems) for which they are seeking help and that you have both had an opportunity to share your views on the type of coaching that might be most helpful to them. I will further assume that you have both agreed to proceed with EPF-CEBC.

Table 7.2 Situational ABCDEFG framework

A = Adversity			

B = Rigid and extreme basic attitudes
 	
Rigid attitude
 	
Extreme attitudes
  - Awfulising attitude
  - Discomfort intolerance attitude
  - Depreciation attitude
	D = Dialectical engagement
	
	---------→
		B = Flexible and non-extreme basic attitudes
		Flexible attitude
		
		Non-extreme attitudes
		  - Non-awfulising attitude
		  - Discomfort tolerance attitude
		  - Acceptance attitude
			F = Facilitating change

C = Disturbed responses (consequences of rigid and extreme basic attitudes) Emotional Behavioural Cognitive	---------→	E = Effects of dialectical engagement C = Healthy responses (consequences of flexible and non-extreme basic attitudes) Emotional Behavioural Cognitive ALSO G = Goals	←-----

7.2.1. Working with the target emotional problem

When your coachee has one emotional problem for which they are seeking help then it is clear that this becomes their "target problem". A target problem in EPF-CEBN is an emotional problem that you and your coachee have agreed to target for change. However, when your coachee has two or more emotional problems that they wish to address it is important to help them deal with these one at a time. Your initial task as coach in such circumstances is to help your coachee to develop a problem list, to understand that it is best to deal with one emotional problem at a time and to select a problem to address first. Once this has been done, the selected problem is again known as the "target problem".

7.2.1.1. Working with a specific example of the target problem

In my view, it is important for you to encourage your coachee to select a specific example of their target problem for you both work with. A specific example increases the chances that your coachee will identify valid, emotionally laden information that will help you both as you help your coachee to effect change. On the other hand, if you discuss your coachee's problem at a general or abstract level then the work will seem theoretical and lacking the emotional engagement that is important to facilitate real change. Thus, ask your coachee to select a specific example of their target problem that is one of the following:

- Recent
- Typical
- Memorable
- Anticipated.

7.2.1.2. Understanding the target problem

Once you have agreed to work with a specific example of your coachee's target problem then you need to assess it using the Situational ABC part of the framework.

7.2.1.2.1. IDENTIFY AND DESCRIBE THE SITUATION IN WHICH THE PROBLEM OCCURRED

Your first step is to have your coachee describe as factually as possible what happened in the situation where the problem occurred. I have given an example of how to do this at the beginning of the chapter when I discussed the coachee who reported feeling hurt when she inferred that a colleague ignored her. If you recall, what actually happened was that your coachee passed their colleague in the street, greeted them, but received no greeting in return.

7.2.1.2.2. IDENTIFY THE COACHEE'S C

At this stage, you need to assess "A" or "C" and the order in which you do this will depend, in part, on how your coachee talks about the example of their target problem. However, my suggestion is that wherever possible start with assessing the emotional "C", because normally this is why your coachee has sought help. Then you can assess the behavioural "C" and the cognitive "C".

7.2.1.2.2.1. Identify the coachee's main emotional C
It is important to realise that your coachee may experience more than one disturbed emotion in the specific episode being assessed. If so, help the person to identify the one main disturbed emotion that they wish to change. When you ask your coachee what their main emotion was in the example of their target problem, they may respond in a number of different ways.

- They may give you a negative emotion that is clearly an unhealthy negative emotion (UNE). In this case you can proceed to identify "A".
- They may give you a negative emotion where it is not clear whether this is an unhealthy negative emotion (UNE) or a healthy negative emotion (HNE). In this case refer to the behaviour and subsequent thinking sections of Appendix 1 and use the relevant information as guides in helping your coachee to make a decision on this point.
- They may give you a vague emotion (e.g. "I felt upset"). In this case ask clarifying questions until a clear UNE has been identified. Use the information in Appendix 1 to help you here if necessary.
- They may give you an inference as an emotion (e.g. "I felt rejected"). In which case ask them how they felt about the inference (e.g. "How did you feel about being rejected?") until a clear UNE has been identified. Again, use Appendix 1 to help you.

7.2.1.2.2.2. Identify the coachee's behavioural C's
Once you have identified the main UNE you can use this to identify their behavioural C's. These include both overt actions and action tendencies. For example, you can ask: "When you felt hurt in this situation what did you do?" If the person does not report any overt actions, ask: "When you felt hurt in this situation what did you feel like doing, but didn't do?"

In addition, as discussed earlier in the chapter, it is important that you help your coachee understand the difference between behaviours that are expressions of their disturbed emotions and behaviours designed to protect them from these emotions.

7.2.1.2.2.3. Identify the coachee's cognitive C's
As noted earlier, cognitive C's are thoughts and images that stem from your coachee's basic attitudes towards the adversity in their problem. When these basic attitudes are rigid and extreme then the content of these cognitive C's are skewed to the negative and highly distorted (see Table 2.1 in Chapter 2) and their style is ruminative in nature. However, when these attitudes are flexible and non-extreme then the cognitive C's are realistic in content and their style is non-ruminative and problem-solving in nature. I will discuss how to deal with highly distorted cognitive C's in later in this chapter.

7.2.1.2.3. IDENTIFY THE COACHEE'S A

Once you have identified your coachee's "C", especially their emotional C, you can use this information to identify what it was about the situation that they felt most disturbed (i.e. their adversity at "A"). There are many ways of doing this. In Table 7.3, I present one such approach, which I have called "Windy's Magic Question". The coach in the following chapter shows how to use it in coaching practice.

Table 7.3 Windy's Magic Question (WMQ)

Purpose: To help the coachee to identify the "A" in the ABC framework as quickly as possible (i.e. what the coachee is most disturbed about) once "C" has been assessed and the situation in which "C" has occurred has been identified and briefly described.

Step 1: Have the coachee focus on their disturbed "C" (e.g. "anxiety").

Step 2: Have the coachee focus on the situation in which "C" occurred (e.g. "about to give a public presentation to a group of consultants").

Step 3: Ask the coachee: "Which ingredient could we give you to eliminate or significantly reduce 'C'"? (here, anxiety). (In this case the coachee said: "my mind not going blank"). Take care that the coachee does not change the situation (i.e. they do not say: "not giving the presentation").

Step 4: The opposite is probably "A" (e.g. "my mind going blank"), but check. Ask: "So when you were about to give the presentation, were you most anxious about your mind going blank?" If not, use the question again until the coachee confirms what they were most anxious about in the described situation.

7.2.1.2.4. HELP YOUR COACHEE TO UNDERSTAND THE B–C CONNECTION AND TO IDENTIFY THEIR TWO SETS OF BASIC ATTITUDES

You are now getting to the heart of the framework that underpins EPF-CEBC. The central view of this framework is that your coachee's emotional problem (at C) is neither determined by the situation in which they experience this problem nor by the adversity (at A) that they are most disturbed about. Rather, your coachee's emotional problem is largely determined by the rigid and extreme basic attitudes that they hold at B towards the adversity. In addition, if your coachee is to be helped to respond healthily (at C) to the adversity (at A), then they need to develop and hold a set of alternative flexible and non-extreme attitudes (at B). The relationship between your coachee's problem/solution at C and their basic attitudes at B is known as the B–C connection.

Your coachee is now ready to be helped to understand both this B–C connection and the specific basic attitudes that underpin their problem and that could underpin the solution to this problem. While there are a variety of ways of doing this, I have developed a method which accomplishes both of these tasks at once. It is called "Windy's Review Assessment Procedure (WRAP)" and I describe its use in the following chapter.

Once you have done this you can also use this method with the one extreme attitude that your coachee thinks is linked most closely to their rigid attitude (i.e. awfulising attitude, discomfort intolerance attitude or depreciation attitude) and its non-extreme attitude alternative (i.e. non-awfulising attitude, discomfort tolerance attitude or acceptance attitude). Of course, you can also use the WRAP method while combining the two sets of attitudes.

7.2.1.2.5. HELP YOUR COACHEE TO SET ADVERSITY-RELATED GOALS

It is important that you help your coachee to have a clear idea of what they are striving towards when addressing their problem. In assessing this problem, you have helped them to identify the emotional, behavioural and cognitive components of their problematic response to the adversity at "A". It is very important that your coachee develops a set of alternative and healthy emotional, behavioural and cognitive responses to the same adversity. These healthy responses will encourage them to attempt to change the adversity at "A" and help them to be in the right frame of mind to do so. Your coachee's attempts to set goals that involve them bypassing the adversity should be discouraged and a clear rationale given for this.

If, after this, your coachee still wants to set goals while bypassing "A", go along with this strategy to preserve the coaching alliance, but monitor closely its effects.

7.2.1.3. Engage your coachee in an examination of their rigid/extreme and flexible/non-extreme attitudes using the dialectical method (at D)

As discussed above, once your coachee understands the B–C connection, particularly as it is manifest in the assessment of their problem and potential solution, the next stage is to help them to examine the rigid and/or extreme basic attitudes that underpin the specific example of their emotional problem and the flexible and/or non-extreme basic attitudes that underpin the potential solution to this problem. This stage is "D" and I have called it "dialectical engagement". This phrase usually refers to a discourse between two or more people holding different points of view about a subject but wishing to establish the truth through reasoned arguments. I have adapted the use of this term to the situation in coaching whereby one person (i.e. your coachee) holds opposing attitudes towards an adversity and wishes to establish, again through reasoned argument, which attitude is truthful, most sensible and most helpful and which is false, least sensible and least helpful.

There are a number of ways of using dialectical engagement in EPF-CEBC. I will mention two here and demonstrate one at length in the following chapter.

7.2.1.3.1. CHOICE-BASED DIALECTICAL ENGAGEMENT

In using choice-based dialectical engagement to help your coachee examine their rigid and extreme attitudes, on the one hand, and their alternative flexible and non-extreme attitudes, on the other, you encourage them to do this by considering them together so that they can more easily discriminate between them on empirical, logical and pragmatic grounds and give reasons for their choice. I describe how to do this in the following chapter.

7.2.1.3.2. TEACH YOUR CHILDREN WELL

Another way of encouraging your coachee to use dialectical engagement while examining their rigid/extreme and flexible/non-extreme attitudes is to ask them to imagine which attitude would they teach their children as part of their upbringing and why they would teach the chosen attitude and why they would not teach the rejected attitude. After doing this, and assuming that your coachee selects the flexible/non-extreme attitude, you can discuss with them what, if any, doubts, reservations or objections they would have in developing this attitude for themself.

7.2.1.4. Acknowledge what has been (and has not been) achieved at E

It is useful to review what has been achieved at this point of the EPF-CEBC process. At E – the effects of dialectical engagement – your coachee should understand the emotional, behavioural and cognitive components of the disturbed response to the adversity that features in their problem. They should know the rigid and/or extreme attitudes that they hold towards the adversity that underpin their problem and the flexible and/or non-extreme alternative attitudes that underpin the solution to their problem. As such, the consequences of their flexible and/or non-extreme attitudes constitute their problem-related goals. Furthermore, they should understand that their rigid and extreme attitudes are false, illogical and unhelpful and that their flexible and non-extreme attitudes are true, logical and helpful and they should know why these are the case.

However, this knowledge, on its own, won't yet make a difference to their actual responses to the adversity in question. What will make such a difference is your coachee acting on this knowledge while facing the adversity and rehearsing their flexible/non-extreme attitudes and doing this as many times as they need to until they have achieved their problem-related goal. This is done at F – facilitating change.

7.2.1.5. Help your coachee to facilitate real change at F

In order to facilitate change, you need to help your coachees to implement a number of cognitive, imagery, behavioural and emotive tasks which will help them achieve their problem-related goals. In this book, I am not going to list and describe a large number of coaching techniques (see Whitten, 2009, for such a text), You should however be guided by a number of important principles.

7.2.1.5.1. INVOLVE YOUR COACHEE IN THE SELECTION OF TASKS

While you can suggest tasks to your coachee from the CEB literature (e.g. Whitten, 2009), involve them in the selection of tasks, particularly focusing on tasks that they have found useful in the past. Remember that effective CEBC concerns the fusion between your expertise and that of your coachee.

7.2.1.5.2. ENCOURAGE YOUR COACHEE TO USE COGNITIVE AND BEHAVIOURAL TASKS IN HARMONY

The best way for your coachee to strengthen a flexible and non-extreme attitude is to act in ways that are consistent with it. Similarly, your coachee's constructive behaviour is likely to persist if it is underpinned by an attitude that they are committed to develop. In this way, healthy attitudes and constructive behaviour are mutually reinforcing. Correspondingly, you need to help your coachee refrain from doing one thing and thinking another since this will perpetuate the existence of their problem.

7.2.1.5.3. ENCOURAGE YOUR COACHEE, WHENEVER FEASIBLE, TO FACE ADVERSITY IN A WAY THAT IS CHALLENGING TO THEM, BUT NOT OVERWHELMING FOR THEM

One of the most robust findings in helping people deal with adversity is that facing it is more effective than avoiding it in the long term, although more uncomfortable in the short term. Consequently, you need to discuss this trade-off with your coachee. While facing an adversity fully is the most efficient way of dealing effectively with it, it may be that your coachee is not prepared to do this.

Consequently, the idea of facing an adversity in a way that your coachee experiences a sense of challenge, but is not overwhelmed by the prospect of doing so, should be introduced to and discussed with your coachee (Dryden, 1985). In this respect, it is important that you remember that the more your coachee commits themself to a freely chosen way of facing the adversity, the more they are likely to do so.

7.2.1.5.4. ENCOURAGE YOUR COACHEE TO CARRY OUT PROPERLY NEGOTIATED HOMEWORK TASKS

EPF-CEBC usually takes place once a week and what your coachee does between coaching sessions is as important as what they do within sessions. Thus, you need to spend some time at the end of a coaching session negotiating a suitable assignment with your coachee. Here are some important points to consider as you do so.

- Ensure that you and your coachee have sufficient time to negotiate a suitable assignment
- Involve your coachee fully in the process and take seriously their own suggestions
- Ensure that the task follows from the work you have done in the coaching session. Thus, the task involved may be a reading assignment, a

cognitive assignment, an imagery assignment, a behavioural or a combined assignment
- Agree with the coachee the purpose of the task and what the coachee hopes to achieve by doing it
- Ensure that it is a task that your coachee has the capability of doing
- Encourage your coachee to commit to doing the task and agree its frequency, where and when they are going to do it
- Identify and problem-solve any predicted obstacles to task execution
- Suggest that your coachee make a written note of the assignment and its purpose and that the note can easily be consulted. Some coaches give their coachees a task assignment record book in which to keep a written record of agreed assignments and their experiences of carrying them out.

7.2.1.5.5. REVIEW HOMEWORK TASKS WITH YOUR COACHEE AT THE BEGINNING OF THE FOLLOWING SESSION

It is important that you review your coachee's experiences of carrying out the agreed assignment at the beginning of the coaching session unless there is a good reason not to do so (e.g. your coachee is in crisis with a different issue). Here are some important points to consider as you do so.

- Check whether or not your coachee did the assignment as agreed
- If so, focus on what they learned from doing the task
- Capitalise on their learning during the session and beyond
- If your coachee made any change to the agreed assignment, explore and discuss the reason for this change. Deal with any obstacles that accounted for an unproductive change. Any productive changes to agreed assignments should be remarked upon
- If your coachee did not do the assignment, explore the reason(s) for this very carefully and identify and deal with the obstacles
- Re-negotiate the assignment if still relevant so that the coachee can gain the experience of addressing the obstacle and doing the assignment.

7.2.1.5.6. ENCOURAGE YOUR COACHEE TO DEAL WITH THEIR HIGHLY DISTORTED COGNITIVE C'S, IF RELEVANT

There are four basic approaches for working with your coachee when they have highly distorted cognitive C's that stem from their rigid and extreme basic attitudes at B about the adversity at A. These are best carried out *after* you and your coachee have engaged in a dialectical discussion about the above rigid and extreme attitudes and their flexible and non-extreme counterparts. The reason for this is that in order to get the most from examining distorted cognitive C's your coachee needs to be in the right, objective frame of mind, which is best achieved when they are not "under the influence" of their rigid and extreme attitudes.

- Help your coachee to understand how they have unwittingly created these highly distorted cognitions by the rigid and extreme attitudes that they hold towards their adversity. Thus, these thoughts at "C" reflect your coachee's attitudes rather than reality. Once your coachee understands this, this will help them to distance themself from these thoughts.
- Help your coachee to question the evidence for and against the highly distorted thought and then to develop one or more realistic alternatives. Have them also question the evidence for and against these alternatives and then encourage them to choose and go with the thought that appears the most realistic.
- Help your coachee to spot the major inferential distortion in the thought under examination and to find an alternative that corrects the distortion (see Table 2.1). Then, suggest that they submit both thoughts to the same empirical analysis described above.
- Teach them how to accept the distorted thought mindfully without either engaging with it or without attempting to eliminate it. This approach is particularly useful if your coachee reports that they are ruminating over the thought in question.

From a pluralistic perspective, you can outline these different approaches and also elicit your coachee's views on how they can deal best with their distorted cognitive C's prior to agreeing the best way forward for them on this issue.

7.2.1.6. Help your coachee to maintain their progress

Remember, at the beginning of EPF-CEBC, you are working with a specific example of your coachee's target problem. For homework, your coachee will be asked to face other examples of the same problem until they make progress on it. Then, you need to help them to maintain their progress by suggesting that they continue to face similar examples that are increasingly more challenging for them. For example, in the next chapter, I will discuss the case of Edward who had a problem with anxiety about meeting people that he did not know. On assessment, this was specifically to do with him being judged negatively as weird. Initially, this was addressed by his coach in the context of him being introduced to people he did not know at parties and he continued to go to parties to face his fears. As he improved, he increased the challenge by introducing himself to strangers and practised his developing flexible and non-extreme attitudes while doing so. He maintained his progress by "avoiding his avoidance" and by going to parties whenever he could and talking to people he did not know.

7.2.1.7. Help your coachee to generalise learning to other problems

It is also important to look for ways in which you can help your coachee to generalise their learning from their target problem to other problems that they are seeking help for. Here the opportunities for generalisation are best presented, initially, when the coachee's rigid and extreme attitudes are the same across problems.

In summary, generalisation is best done when it is underpinned by the relevant healthy flexible and non-extreme attitudes.

In the next chapter, I will discuss in full how Lena, a CEB coach, helped Edward who came to coaching for help with an anxiety problem about meeting people he did not know in social settings. In doing so, I will refer to many of the points discussed in this chapter.

Notes

1 Negative healthy emotions about adversities, while healthy in consequence, are negative in feeling tone because adversities are themselves negative. In effect, what I am saying is that it is healthy to feel bad, but not disturbed about an adversity.
2 In this chapter, I am mainly addressing your coachee's emotional problem. However, what I have to say about understanding and dealing with this problem also applies to the situations a) where your coachee has a disturbed response to the practical problem for which they are seeking help and b) where they have a disturbed response to a coaching-related obstacle.
3 I will discuss and illustrate goal-setting in relation to your coachee's emotional problem in the following chapter.

Chapter 8

Edward: an example of emotional problem-focused cognitive-emotive-behavioural coaching (EPF-CEBC)

In this chapter, I will discuss the case of Edward, a 29-year-old, single, computer software manager. Edward was ambitious and realised that to improve the chances of job advancement he needed to tackle his anxiety problem about meeting new people in social situations related to work. He was expected to socialise with potential new clients at promotional social events and was struggling to do this. Because he did not want his employer to know of this problem, he decided to seek help from an external coach and to fund the work himself.

8.1. The brief real-time initial screening conversation with Edward

At the brief 10-minute phone conversation that Edward had with Lena, the coach he found online, she discovered the following:

- Edward wanted to address his anxiety problem, as outlined above.
- He contacted Lena because she said on her website that she specialised in coaching for social anxiety problems.
- He was looking for coaching to solve his problem and put no time constraints on this.
- He was self-funding and Lena's fee was within his budget.
- He did not want anyone at his work to know that he would be having coaching.

From what Edward told Lena, she said to him that she thought that he might be a good candidate for emotional problem-focused coaching (EPF-CEBC) and that they should meet for a face-to-face session to see if this was the case and to make a contract if they decided to work with one another. Edward agreed.

8.2. Assessing Edward for CEBC and contracting with him

At the face-to-face meeting, Lena began by assessing Edward's anxiety problem and found that it met most of Cavanagh's (2005) criteria. Although it was not of recent origin, it was moderately distressing to Edward. It was limited to a certain aspect of Edwards's life and he was not defensive about it. Finally, Edward was open to address and change the problem. Thus it was clear that Edward was a good candidate for emotional problem-focused coaching, and when Lena explained to him about CEBC he thought that it would be helpful to him. In addition, Edward and Lena negotiated a contract with respect to confidentiality (with Lena stressing that she would not inform his employers about him having coaching), the open-ended nature of coaching, her fees and how they would be paid, Lena's cancellation policy, her referral policy and their respective roles and responsibilities.

8.3. Working with Edward's target emotional problem

Edward came to coaching at the outset with one problem which automatically became his target problem. This was: "I get anxious about meeting new people in social situations related to work." Initially, Edward stated that he wanted to "get over" his anxiety problem. When asked about their goals with respect to emotional problems, often coachees just want the problem to be gone. As such, it is often best to wait until a more detailed assessment of the problem before discussing goals in more detail. This was the stance taken by Lena with Edward.

8.3.1. Working with a specific example of Edward's target problem

As noted in Chapter 7, it is important for you to work with a specific example of your coachee's target problem. Doing so helps you both understand the specifics of their problem and thus facilitates the change process because your coachee will be working with emotionally laden experience. This represents the "E" in CEBC. A specific example can be recent, typical, memorable or anticipated. Edward chose a recent example of his problem.

8.3.1.1. Understanding Edward's target problem

Once Lena and Edward agreed to work with a specific recent example of Edward's target problem, then she assessed it using the Situational ABC part of the Situational ABCDEFG framework.

8.3.1.1.1. EDWARD IDENTIFIES AND DESCRIBES THE SITUATION IN WHICH THE PROBLEM OCCURRED

Lena's first step was to have Edward describe as factually as possible what happened in the situation where the problem occurred.

Edward chose the following situation, which provided the context for the specific recent example of his target problem of feeling anxious about meeting new people: "Going to a work-sponsored party and being introduced to someone I don't know."

8.3.1.1.2. HELPING EDWARD TO IDENTIFY C

At this stage, Lena needs to assess Edward's "A" or "C" and the order in which she does this depends, in part, on how Edward talks about the example of his target problem. As Edward started talking about his emotions at "C", Lena took his lead. Then, she assessed the behavioural "C" and the cognitive "C".

8.3.1.1.2.1. Identifying Edward's main emotional C. As already mentioned, Edward's "C" was anxiety.

8.3.1.1.2.2. Identifying Edward's behavioural C's. Once Lena identified Edward's main unhealthy negative emotion (UNE), which was anxiety, she used this to identify his behavioural C's.

Edward's behavioural C's in the example were to avoid being introduced to new people at the party or, if he could not avoid it, to withdraw as quickly as possible from talking to them once introduced.

8.3.1.1.2.3. Identifying Edward's cognitive C's. Edward's cognitive C's are the thoughts and images that he had in the situation that stemmed from his basic attitudes toward the adversity ("A") in his problem. As these basic attitudes were likely to be rigid and extreme, then the content of Edward's cognitive C's are likely to be skewed to the negative and highly distorted.

Edward's cognitive C's in the example were: "When people who I meet think I'm weird, they will tell other people" and "I'm never going to get over this problem."

Often when your coachee reveals their cognitive C's they may also reveal what their "A" is. As we shall see, this was the case with Edward.

8.3.1.1.3. IDENTIFYING EDWARD'S "A"

Once Lena identified Edward's "C", especially his emotional C, she used this information to identify what it was about the situation that Edward felt most anxious about.

So far Edward has given Lena the following information that will be particularly helpful to her in the assessment of "A":

- Situation: Going to a work-related party and being introduced to someone I don't know
- C (emotional) = Anxiety

Simple questions Lena could have asked to identify Edward's "A" were "What is most anxiety-provoking for you about being introduced to someone you don't know at the work-related party?" or "When you are introduced to someone you don't know at the work-related party, what are you most anxious about?"

However, Lena used a technique I developed called "Windy's Magic Question" (WMQ) – see Chapter 7. Here are the steps she took with Edward.

- *Step 1:* She had Edward focus on his disturbed emotional "C" (e.g. "anxiety").
- *Step 2:* She had Edward focus on the situation in which "C" occurred or is predicted to occur (in this case: "being introduced to someone I don't know at the work-related party").
- *Step 3:* She asked Edward: "Which ingredient could we give you to eliminate or significantly reduce your anxiety?" Edward replied: "The person not thinking that I'm weird if I dry up." If Edward changed the situation (e.g. he said "not going to the party" or "avoiding being introduced to strangers"), then Lena would have encouraged him to imagine that he was at the party and that he could not avoid being introduced to strangers.
- *Step 4:* The opposite is probably "A" (e.g. "The person thinking I'm weird if I dry up"), but Lena checked. She asked: "So if you are about to be introduced to someone you don't know at the work-related party, are you most anxious about them thinking you are weird if you dry up?" If Edward had said no, then Lena would have used the question again until Edward confirmed what he was most anxious about in the described situation.

Edward confirmed that his "A" was: "The person thinking I'm weird if I dry up."

8.3.1.1.4. HELPING EDWARD TO UNDERSTAND THE B–C CONNECTION AND TO IDENTIFY HIS TWO SETS OF BASIC ATTITUDES

The central view of the framework that underpins EPF-CEBC is that Edward's anxiety problem (at C) is neither determined by the situation in which he experiences this problem nor by the adversity (at A) that he is most disturbed about. Rather, Edward's emotional problem is largely determined by the rigid and extreme basic attitudes that he holds at B towards the adversity. In addition, if Lena is to help Edward to respond healthily (at C) to the adversity (at A), then she needs to help him to develop and hold a set of alternative flexible and non-extreme attitudes (at B). The relationship between Edward's problem/solution at C and his basic attitudes at B is known as the B–C connection.

Lena helped Edward to understand i) this B–C connection and ii) the specific basic attitudes that both underpin their problem and those that could underpin the solution to this problem by using a method that I developed which accomplishes both of these tasks at once. It is called "Windy's Review Assessment Procedure" (WRAP), and here is how she used it with Edward.

- **Step 1**: Lena said: "Let's review what we know and what we don't know so far."
- **Step 2**: She said: "We know four things. First, we know that you were anxious ('C'). Second, we know that you were anxious about the stranger that you were introduced to thinking that you were weird if you dried up ('A'). Third, we know that your goal with respect to the problem is to address your anxiety[1] about this adversity, and fourth – and this is an educated guess on my part – we know that it is important to you that the stranger does not think of you as weird if you dried up. Am I correct?"

  Edward confirmed Lena's hunch. Note that what she has done is to identify the part of the attitude that is common to both Edward's rigid basic attitude and his alternative flexible basic attitude, as we will see.
- **Step 3**: Lena then said: "Now let's review what we don't know. This is where I need your help. We don't know which of two attitudes your anxiety was based on. So, when you were anxious about the stranger thinking that you were weird if you dried up, was your anxiety based on Attitude 1: 'It is important to me that the stranger does not think I'm weird if I dry up and therefore they must not do so' ('Rigid attitude') or Attitude 2: 'It is important to me that the stranger does not think I'm weird if I dry up, but that does not mean that they must not do so' ('Flexible attitude')?"
- **Step 4**: If necessary, if he was unsure, Lena would have helped Edward to understand that his anxiety was based on his rigid attitude.
- **Step 5**: Once Edward was clear that his anxiety was based on his rigid attitude, Lena made and emphasised the rigid attitude–disturbed "C" connection. Then she asked: "Now let's suppose instead that you had a strong conviction in Attitude 2, how would you feel about the stranger at the party thinking that you were weird if you dried up if you strongly believed that while it was important to you that they did not think that you were weird if you dried up, it did not follow that they must not do so?"
- **Step 6**: If necessary, Lena would have helped Edward to understand that this attitude would help him to feel concerned but not anxious about the adversity, and if she had not already done so, she would have suggested that this could be his goal with respect to the problem. In doing so, she would have made and emphasised the flexible attitude–healthy "C" connection.
- **Step 7**: Lena helped Edward to understand clearly the differences between the two B–C connections.
- **Step 8**: Lena helped Edward commit to un-anxious concern as his emotional goal in this situation and encouraged him to see that developing conviction in his flexible attitude was the best way of achieving this goal.

Once she did that, she also used this method with the one extreme attitude that Edward thought was linked most closely to his rigid attitude (in this case a self-depreciation attitude) and its non-extreme attitude alternative (in this case a self-acceptance attitude).

8.3.1.2. How Lena helped Edward to set problem-related goals

In using WRAP (see above), Lena put forward the idea to Edward that "concern" was the healthy emotional alternative to "anxiety". Before moving on to engage Edward in a dialectical discussion of his two sets of attitudes, Lena encouraged Edward to be more explicit about his problem-related goal. If you recall from our discussion in Chapter 7, emotional problem-related goal-setting is best done in the context of the person's adversity ("A") which, in Edward's case, was "a stranger thinking I'm weird if I dry up". So, Lena first established that Edward could see that "concern" was a heathier and more realistic alternative to anxiety at "C" with respect to the adversity happening at "A". Edward confirmed that it was. Thus, concern could also be seen as emotional goal at "G" in the Situational ABCDEFG framework.

Second, Lena helped Edward to set behavioural goals at "C". Thus, instead of avoiding being introduced to strangers at work-related social events or withdrawing from them at the earliest opportunity if he could not avoid such introductions, Edward set the following behavioural goals which accompanied his emotional goal of "concern": "to face being introduced to strangers at work-related social events and to remain speaking to them". These can also be seen as Edward's behavioural goals at "G".

Finally, Lena helped Edward to set cognitive goals at "C" which again accompanied his emotional goal of "concern". Thus, when he thought, "When people think I'm weird they will tell other people," he would accept this thought, but respond in a more balanced way ("If people I meet think I'm weird, some might tell other people, but most won't"). Also, when he thought, "I'm never going to get over this problem," he would again accept the thought but respond in the same balanced manner ("I might not get over this problem, but if I apply myself, with help, I can probably do so").

These more balanced thoughts can also be seen as his cognitive goals at G.

8.3.1.3. How Lena engaged Edward in a dialectical examination of his rigid/extreme and flexible/non-extreme attitudes (at D)

Once Lena helped Edward to understand the B–C connection, particularly with respect to the attitudes that underpinned his problem and potential solution and clarified his goals, Lena's next task was to help Edward examine the rigid and/or extreme basic attitudes that underpinned the specific example of his target emotional problem and the flexible and/or non-extreme basic attitudes that underpinned the potential solution to this problem. In this book, I refer to this as "dialectical engagement" at D, as it refers to the situation where, in this case, Edward holds opposing attitudes towards an adversity and where Lena engages him in a discussion based on reasoned argument to establish which attitude is truthful, most sensible and most helpful and which is false, least sensible and least helpful.

There are a number of ways of using dialectical engagement in EPF-CEBC. Lena used what I call "choice-based engagement".

8.3.1.3.1. CHOICE-BASED DIALECTICAL ENGAGEMENT

In using choice-based dialectical engagement to help Edward examine his rigid attitude, on the one hand, and his alternative flexible attitude, on the other, Lena asked Edward to consider them together so that he could more easily discriminate between them on empirical, logical and pragmatic grounds and to give reasons for their choice (see below).

LENA: So now let me help you to question both attitudes. I am going to ask you to write both attitudes down and then focus on them while I ask you some questions. OK?

EDWARD: OK.

LENA: So, if you focus on both attitudes, namely Attitude 1: "It is important to me that the stranger does not think I'm weird if I dry up and therefore they must not do so" or Attitude 2: "It is important to me that the stranger does not think I'm weird if I dry up, but that does not mean that they must not do so?", which idea is true and which is false?

EDWARD: The first one is false and the second one is true.

LENA: Why?

EDWARD: Well the second one recognises what's important to me but also recognises that I don't have to get what's important to me. That's how the world works. If I ran the world then I would arrange that it would not be possible for any person I had just met to think that I was weird. But that is not reality and the second attitude recognises that. That's why the first one is false. It states that I have to get what I want, but I don't. In fact, the more I demand that I get what is important to me, in this case the stranger not thinking I'm weird, the more anxious I will become and the more likely it is that the person will pick up on my anxiety and judge me as weird.

LENA: OK. Now which of these attitudes is logical or sensible and which is illogical or nonsensical?

EDWARD: Well, Attitude 1 does not make sense as it is illogical to think that I have to get something just because I want it. Attitude 2 does make sense as it acknowledges what I want, but also recognises that I don't have to get what I want.

LENA: Finally, which attitude is helpful to you and which is unhelpful?

EDWARD: Attitude 1 is definitely unhelpful because it is giving me the very problem I want to address. Attitude 2 gives me the opportunity to feel concerned, but not anxious, about the prospect about being thought to be weird. This emotion would not lead me to avoid work-based social settings or to be desperate to get out of being introduced to people I don't know.

Then Lena used the choice-based dialectical method to help Edward examine his self-depreciation attitude, on the one hand, and his alternative unconditional self-acceptance on the other, with similar productive results.

8.3.1.4. Helping Edward to acknowledge what has been (and has not been) achieved at E

At this point, Lena reviewed what Edward had achieved so far. At E – the effects of the dialectical engagement – Edward understood what were the emotional, behavioural and cognitive components of his problematic response to the prospect of being thought weird by someone he just met if he dried up. He knew that the rigid and self-depreciation attitudes that he held towards this adversity underpinned his problem and that the flexible and unconditional self-acceptance alternative attitudes underpinned the solution to his problem. As such, the consequences of his flexible and unconditional self-acceptance attitudes constituted his problem-related goal.

Furthermore, Edward understood that his rigid and self-depreciation attitudes were false, illogical and unhelpful and that his flexible and self-acceptance attitudes were true, logical and helpful, and he knew the reasons why these were the case.

8.3.1.5. Helping Edward to facilitate real change at F

As discussed in Chapter 7, Edward's understanding of these points, on its own, won't yet make a difference to his actual responses to the prospect of being thought weird by someone he has just met if he dries up. What will make such a difference is Edward acting on this knowledge when facing the adversity in question while rehearsing his flexible/unconditional self-acceptance attitudes and doing this as many times as he needs to until he has achieved his problem-related goal. This is done at F – facilitating change.

8.3.1.5.1. INVOLVING EDWARD IN THE SELECTION OF CHANGE-RELATED TASKS

Lena suggested a number of tasks that Edward might consider to facilitate change and also encouraged him to suggest his own. They agreed that the best way forward was for Edward to think and act in ways that strengthened his flexible and unconditional self-acceptance attitudes. In this case to go to at least one work-related social event a week and ask to be introduced to people he did not know while rehearsing a short-hand version of an unconditional self-acceptance attitude: "I'm not weird even if they think I am. I'm human." To start with, Edward agreed to be introduced to one stranger per event, then two, then three etc., the increase being dependent on the increase in his confidence. In this way, Edward took a "challenging, but not overwhelming" approach to addressing his emotional problem (Dryden, 1985).

8.3.1.5.2 NEGOTIATING AND REVIEWING HOMEWORK TASKS WITH EDWARD

Edward was very diligent in carrying out the tasks related to the change-related plan mentioned above, so that Lena did not have to perform many of the tasks that a coach performs with respect to homework assignments (see Chapter 7).

Edward generally did stick to the plan and found it easier to do than he initially thought. He learned three major things from implementing the plan. First, when he did dry up, others were adept at helping him to reconnect to the conversation. Second, the more he faced what he thought was an adversity, the more he saw that he was overestimating the adversity. People were much kinder than he had ever imagined. Third, the more he talked to strangers, the more confident he got at speaking with them.

8.3.1.5.3. DEALING WITH EDWARD'S OBSTACLE TO CHANGE

The only obstacle Edward encountered along the way was that occasionally he backed away from opportunities of being introduced to a stranger when he thought that the person was very confident. In his view, a confident person would be more likely to think that he was weird if he dried up in conversation. Lena helped him here in two ways. First, she showed him that far from being a bad thing, if it were true that a confident person would be more likely to think that he was weird than someone not as confident, then this was a good thing because it gave him an opportunity to face his fear head on and practise his newly acquired flexible and unconditional self-acceptance attitudes. Second, Lena encouraged Edward to implement his own suggestion that it was worth it for him to tolerate the increased discomfort of speaking to confident strangers at work-related social events and that he could do so. With these two strategies, Edward dealt effectively with this obstacle.

8.3.1.5.4. HOW EDWARD DEALT WITH HIS HIGHLY DISTORTED COGNITIVE C's

If you recall, when Edward held rigidly to the attitude that strangers must not think he was weird and, if they did, that proved he was weird, he made himself anxious about meeting strangers at work-related social events and under the influence of this anxiety he thought:

- "When people who I meet think I'm weird, they will tell other people" and
- "I'm never going to get over this problem."

These thoughts were cognitive consequences (at "C") of his rigid and self-depreciation attitudes.

First, Lena helped Edward to see that these thoughts were not necessarily reflections of reality, but rather reflections of these attitudes, and that he could distance himself from these thoughts, observe them and remind himself of their origins.

Then, she helped him to put in place the cognitive goals he previously set. These were:

- "If people I meet think I'm weird, some might tell other people, but most won't."
- "I might not get over this problem, but if I apply myself, with help, I can probably do so."

Lena helped Edward to question the evidence for and against both sets of thoughts and then encouraged him to choose and go with the thoughts that appeared the most realistic – which were the latter.

8.3.1.6. How Lena helped Edward to maintain progress

At the beginning of EPF-CEBC, Lena and Edward worked with a specific example of Edward's target anxiety problem. He then applied what he learned to other examples of the same problem until he made progress on it. Then, Lena helped Edward to maintain his progress by suggesting that he face similar examples that were increasingly more challenging for him. As Edward improved, he increased the challenge by getting invitations to prestigious work-related social events and introducing himself to high-status people he did not know and engage them in conversation. While doing this he practised his developing flexible and self-acceptance attitudes.

8.3.1.7. Outcome

Edward did not have any other problem that he wanted to address, so Lena did not need to help him to generalise his gains to other problems. He decided to leave coaching when he "felt" that he had gotten what he came for – gains which he had maintained at a four-month follow-up session. Edward did not want to use any quantitative rating scales, preferring a more felt-sense approach to outcome evaluation. All in all, Edward had 20 sessions of coaching. Initially, these sessions occurred at weekly intervals, but as Edward made more progress, they took place at fortnightly and then monthly intervals.

In the next two chapters, I focus on development-focused CEBC (DF-CEBC) and discuss the salient issues that need to be considered when helping coachees to achieve their development-based objectives.

Note

1 If you have already helped your coachee to set a specific goal with respect to their problem, make specific reference to it at this point.

Chapter 9

A framework to guide and implement cognitive-emotive-behavioural coaching for development (DF-CEBC)

Development-focused cognitive-emotive-behavioural coaching (DF-CEBC), as the name makes clear, is coaching that is focused on helping coachees to develop themselves. Such development is conceptualised in coaching using a variety of terms (e.g. growth, self-actualisation, flourishing). By development I mean where coachees seek to get the most out of themselves in nominated life domains (e.g. work, relationships, personal life). In my view, it is useful for CEBC coaches to have a framework to help them and their coachees think about areas of coachee development and how to foster it.

9.1. Principles to guide coaching for development

In my view, the approach within CEBC that has the most to offer development-focused CEBC, in that it provides coaches with a set of principles for coachee development, is Rational Emotive Behavioural Coaching (REBC). Its founder, Albert Ellis, not only put forward a set of concepts and principles that aids you as a CEBC coach when you come to help your coachees deal with their emotional problems in living (in EPF-CEBC) and address their problematic responses to obstacles to the pursuit of their development-based objectives (in DF-CEBC) – see Chapters 7 and 11 – he also provided a framework of principles that underpins coachee development. In this section of the chapter, I will outline and discuss these principles, which you can introduce to your coachees as a way of facilitating a discussion with them about what they want to get from coaching and in which areas of life they would like to develop themselves.

9.1.1. Personal responsibility

It is important that your coachees accept full responsibility for their responses to life events and for whether or not they initiate a process of self-development. In dealing with problems (in PF-CEBC) and problematic responses to obstacles (in DF-CEBC), taking responsibility means that your coachee accepts that they are largely responsible for their responses to the adversities that provide the context for the problem in the first case and the obstacle in the second case. Assuming such responsibility does not mean that your coachee dismisses the role of the adversity in their problem/problematic response. Rather, it means that your coachee acknowledges the contributory role of the adversity to their problem/problematic response, but fully recognises that their cognitive processing of the adversity plays a more important role in the development and maintenance of the problem/problematic response. As the quote attributed to Epictetus makes clear, "People are disturbed not by things, but by the views they take of them."

In the development phase of DF-CEBC, it is important that your coachee takes responsibility for i) selecting meaningful objectives; ii) devising suitable action plans to facilitate action towards the achievement of these objectives; iii) taking objective-achievement action; and iv) maintaining and enhancing the gains once the objectives have been achieved.

Coaches should recognise that when coachees fail to take responsibility in either PF-CEBC or DF-CEBC, then their first response may be to provide excuses for this, by putting the responsibility either on others (e.g. "She stopped me from doing it") or on the situation (e.g. "It was too cold for me to go to the gym"). Another problem is when the person takes the responsibility, but with self-blame (e.g. "Yes, I did fail to get up when the alarm went off. I am such a lazy good for nothing!").

Your task as CEBC coach is to help coachees to take responsibility without self-blame and to respond to failures to take responsibility with compassionate, corrective action.

9.1.2. Flexible and non-extreme attitudes

Your coachees are much more likely to get the most out of their lives if they hold a set of flexible and non-extreme attitudes than if they hold a set of rigid and extreme attitudes. This is certainly true if they hold a set of flexible and non-extreme attitudes about life's adversities. While these attitudes will lead your coachees to be dissatisfied, but not disturbed, about the existence of adversity, this dissatisfaction will motivate your coachees to take helpful constructive action if the adversity can be changed and to adjust constructively if the adversity cannot be changed.

It is also true that holding flexible and non-extreme attitudes will help your coachee to strive towards development-based growth when they are adversity free. Thus, these attitudes will encourage your coachee to implement their action plans, to maintain their constructive behaviour over time and to deal productively with any obstacles to the pursuit of their development-focused objectives.

When your coachees' attitudes are flexible and non-extreme, they acknowledge that they have desires, but don't transform these into rigid demands on self, others and life conditions. They acknowledge badness, but don't awfulise; they tolerate discomfort when it is in their healthy interests to do so, and they unconditionally accept themselves and other human beings and life as a complex mixture of the good, the bad and the neutral. Holding flexible and non-extreme attitudes, in short, helps your coachee to be open to change and to be minimally defensive.

9.1.3. Scientific thinking and non-utopian in outlook

When your coachees tend to be scientific in their thinking, they regulate their emotions and actions by reflecting on them and by evaluating their consequences with respect to whether or not they lead to the attainment of their development-based objectives. Also, as discussed above, scientific thinking will help your coachees to view their inferences as hunches about reality rather than as facts, and are prepared to examine the accuracy of these inferences by looking at the available evidence.

Such scientific thinking will also help your coachees to be sceptical and not to accept as true assertions that appear attractive or because an authority states that they are true. Thus, scientifically inclined coachees tend to have an independent mind.

Finally, coachees' scientific outlook encourages them to accept the fact that utopias are probably unachievable and also to recognise that it is unlikely that they will get everything they want and that they will frequently experience frustration in their lives.

9.1.4. Unconditional self-acceptance

Unconditional self-acceptance (USA) is an attitude that your coachee takes towards themself that involves them acknowledging that they are too complex to merit a global evaluation of their personhood. Rather, they accept that they are human, alive, fallible, unrateable, complex and in flux and that these are facts about themself that do not change. If they wish to value themself then they are encouraged to make their value dependent on these facts (as they do not change) and not by such things as their extrinsic achievements or others' views of them (which do change).

Contrary to common misconception, USA does not advocate resignation. It encourages your coachee to recognise, without defensiveness, that they may have aspects about themself that they don't like and wish to change, and thence go about the difficult business of changing it, if it can be changed, or accepting without liking it, if it can't be changed.

Also, USA does not encourage your coachee to rest on their laurels. On the contrary, it encourages them to develop themself in the knowledge that they can better themself (i.e. get more out of themself) without becoming a better person (in the sense that their value increases according to how much self-development they achieve).

This attitude helps your coachee to feel glad to be alive. They attempt to enjoy rather than to prove themself and as such they are more likely to follow their own path in life than to follow others, or do what they believe they should do but really don't want to do. A philosophy of unconditional self-acceptance helps your coachee to prioritise themself (see below) and to keep pursuing their objectives even when others criticise them or depreciate them, for example.

9.1.5. Enlightened self-interest

Engaging in the coaching process means that your coachee is called upon to focus on themself and to consider in which areas of life they wish to develop themself. In order to do this, they need to be first and primarily interested in themselves and to put their own healthy interests at least a little above the interests of others. Such self-interest is best founded on a philosophy of unconditional self-acceptance (see above) if it is to prompt committed action over time. Here your coachee accepts themself as a fallible human being equal in worth to others and realises that unless they look after their best interests nobody else will. Having enlightened self-interest does not mean, however, that your coachee is not prepared to sacrifice themself, to some degree, for those for whom they care. However, within the overall context of a philosophy of enlightened self-interest, such self-sacrifice tends to be temporary and boundaried.

Enlightened self-interest (sometimes referred to as self-care) is often mistakenly seen as selfishness, but this is far from the case. Selfishness is a stance whereby your coachee routinely and cynically puts their interests before those of others and does not care about whether or not others miss out on what is important to them as a consequence. By contrast, enlightened self-interest is a flexible position where most of the time your coachee will put their interests first, but some of the time they will put others' interests before their own. In selfishness, care for others is absent, whereas in enlightened self-interest it is present.

9.1.6. Unconditional other-acceptance

I discussed the importance of unconditional self-acceptance above. Unconditional other-acceptance (UOA) is the same attitude but held towards others. This involves your coachee acknowledging that others are too complex to merit a global evaluation of their personhood. Rather, they accept others as human, alive, fallible, unrateable, complex and in flux and that these are facts about these others that do not change. Such an attitude will help your coachee develop better relationships with others.

9.1.7. Social interest

Having enlightened self-interest does not preclude your coachee from also demonstrating social interest, and unconditional other-acceptance will help promote it. Social interest means that they realise that if they do not act morally to protect the rights of others and abet social survival, it is unlikely that they will help to create the kind of world in which they themself can live comfortably and happily. But it more often means your coachee taking an interest in others because they genuinely care about what happens to them. As we shall see, one of the values that underpins a number of coachees' selected development-based objectives is "helping others" or "making a difference to the welfare of others".

9.1.8. Self-direction in a social context

I mentioned earlier that being able to take responsibility is an important principle. Doing so means that your coachee is largely self-directing while simultaneously preferring to co-operate with others. In doing so, they do not need the support or help of others, although they regard these as being desirable. They are not proud to ask for help when they need to and do not regard themselves as weak for doing so. This principle is particularly important in business coaching, where cooperating with others is often important to the achievement of self-directed, development-based goals.

9.1.9. Uncertainty tolerance

There is much in life that is uncertain and therefore it is important that your coachee develops tolerance for uncertainty and does not demand that they must know what is going to happen to them or to others. It is particularly important that your coachee tolerates uncertainty when it comes to the coaching process, especially in its development-focused phase. As your coachee sets off on the journey towards their development-focused objectives, they are venturing into the unknown when it comes to how others are likely to respond to them when they present new facets of themself to the world. Coaching is about coachee change, and while your coachee may predict a favourable response to their new behaviour from others, ultimately they cannot be sure about this. A coachee who demands certainty will seek much reassurance from you and others and this will ultimately lead to them becoming increasingly fearful of taking risks, as this means venturing into the unknown. For this reason, helping your coachee to develop uncertainty tolerance is a key task, particularly in DF-CEBC.

9.1.10. Strong commitment to meaningful objectives

When discussing with your coachee what benefits they wish to derive from DF-CEBC, it is important that you explore with them how meaningful their objectives are to them. The more meaningful their objectives are, the more likely it is that they will be committed to pursuing them. Your coachee will tend to be healthier and happier when they are vitally absorbed in something outside of themself. You may not have anything relevant to say about what these meaningful pursuits should be, as there is an enormous range of such activities available to people. Your task, here, is to encourage your coachee to be themself and go for what they find meaningful no matter how strange this may appear to others. However, you do need to encourage your coachee to be mindful of the reactions of others (see the section on social interest above).

9.1.11. Calculated risk-taking

People who play safe in life may do so for a number of reasons. Often, for example, it is a way of managing anxiety. Here, people act to avoid the anxiety that they would feel if they took a risk and exposed themselves to possible adversity (e.g. failure). Coachees who get the most out of DF-CEBC are those who tend to take a fair number of risks and try to do what they want to do even where there's a good chance that they might fail. They tend to be adventurous, but not foolhardy, in this respect and act on the maxim "nothing ventured, nothing gained".

9.1.12. Discomfort tolerance

Discomfort tolerance is one of the non-extreme attitudes that I discussed above in the section entitled "Flexible and non-extreme attitudes". However, in my view, it is so important in development-focused CEBC, in particular, that it warrants a separate section. Thus, if your coachee has an attitude of discomfort tolerance, then they acknowledge the struggle involved in dealing with discomfort, but recognise that they can tolerate it. Then they act on this attitude if they see that tolerating discomfort is in their interests to do, that they are willing to do so and, most importantly, that they are going to do so. Without this attitude your coachee will be guided by the short-range hedonistic concerns of freeing themself from discomfort and involving themself with pleasurable activities which will not sustain them for very long. Consequently, they will not be successful in achieving their development-based objectives.

9.1.13. Long-range hedonism

When your coachee operates according to the principle of long-range hedonism, as opposed to short-range hedonism, they are prepared to forgo short-term pleasures when these interfere with the pursuit of their long-term development-focused objectives. However, cognitive-emotive-behavioural coaching is no killjoy approach to coaching and you can, thus, encourage your coachee to enjoy themself when doing so has no adverse long-term implications.

9.1.14. Resilience

Resilience is currently a hot topic in positive psychology and coaching; it is therefore important to be clear with your coachee about its nature, as a number of misconceptions exist about the concept (Neenan, 2017). Thus, resilience is not about your coachee being resistant to adversity, not being affected when a stressor is encountered. Neither is it about "bouncing back" to the state that your coachee was in prior to encountering the adversity. Rather, when your coachee demonstrates resilience: first, they allow themself to respond in whatever way they respond to the adversity even if the response is a disturbed one; second, they face and process the experience rather than avoiding it; and finally, they are changed by the experience in productive ways. Thus, they may report that, as a result of the experience, they have a deeper appreciation of what is important to them, they have inner resources they did not know they had, they demonstrate a greater wisdom about life and experience and show a greater compassion for others facing adversity. Finally, their key relationships change for the better. In short, they experience what Joseph (2013) refers to as "post-traumatic growth".

As your coachee needs to face adversity if they wish to develop resilience, your job is to encourage them to take calculated risks (see above), which will increase their chances of dealing effectively with the adversity.

9.1.15. Unconditional life-acceptance (ULA)

Unconditional life-acceptance (ULA) involves your coachee acknowledging that life is an ongoing process and is a complex mixture of a myriad of positive, negative and neutral aspects far too complex to merit a global evaluation. This philosophy will help your coachee to deal with any adversities that occur during DF-CEBC. Here I use the development-based version of the Serenity Prayer: "Unconditional life-acceptance will help me a) to identify obstacles to the pursuit of my objectives; b) to change those obstacles I can change; c) to accept without liking those obstacles I cannot change; and d) to have the wisdom to know the difference."

9.1.16. A process view of life

Your coachee has sought development-focused CEBC presumably because they want to develop themself in certain areas of their life. While an important part of the coaching process is to help them to set objectives, it is also to help them understand that even when they have achieved these objectives this is not the end of the story. Far from it! Once achieved, objectives need to be maintained and even enhanced. Encouraging your coachee to take a process view of life will help them to see that development occurs over the course of life and not just during the life of their coaching relationship with you. It follows, therefore, that you need to help them adopt what I call a self-helping philosophy.

9.1.17. A self-helping philosophy

In development-focused CEBC one of your tasks as a coach is to help your coachee to become their own coach. Paraphrasing a famous Chinese proverb: "You help a coachee to achieve an objective and you nourish them in that area of their life during coaching. You teach them how to achieve their own objectives and you give them a self-helping process that will nourish them for a lifetime." This involves you encouraging the person to learn how to set their own objectives, develop their own action plans and learn to deal with practical and emotional obstacles that they may encounter along the way to reaching their objectives. Then you can help them to maintain and enhance their gains and then to generalise these skills to other life areas. In order for all this to occur your coachee needs to acquire a self-helping philosophy where they believe in the importance of learning to become their own coach. It should be borne in mind, however, that not all coachees are interested in doing this.

9.1.18. Realism

It is useful to encourage your client to adopt a realistic approach to development-focused CEBC. This need to be done carefully because in helping your coachee face the reality of striving towards their objectives you don't want to discourage them. On the other hand, you don't want them to think that everything in the coaching garden will be rosy. Helping your coachee to be realistic about coaching involves them understanding that the process of coaching is like the course of true love – rarely smooth. While they may start with enthusiasm, this may wane particularly if they encounter obstacles along the way. If they are prepared for such eventualities, then they are more likely to benefit from DF-CEBC than if they are not.

9.1.19. A problem-solving mindset

Given that your coachee is likely to experience problems along the way to achieving their objectives, it is useful if you help them to develop a problem-solving mindset. This involves recognising that they may face problems but that by applying a sound problem-solving methodology, these problems may be surmounted. There are many problem-solving frameworks that you can teach your coachees. I have already introduced you to the PRACTICE model developed by Palmer (2008), which I personally use with my coachees.

Nezu, Maguth Nezu & D'Zurilla (2013: 11) talk about helping people to develop a "positive problem orientation". When this is present the person is able to "a) Appraise problems as challenges; b) Be optimistic in believing that problems are solvable; c) Have a strong sense of self-efficacy regarding their ability to cope with problems; d) Understand that successful problem-solving involves time and effort; and e) View negative emotions as an integral part of the overall problem-solving process that can ultimately be helpful in coping with stressful problems". Helping coachees to develop such a mindset will enhance their success at dealing effectively with the obstacles that they encounter in DF-CEBC and is also useful in PF-CEBC.

9.1.20. Strengths and resources

When somebody comes for coaching help it is tempting to look at what they are not doing, to focus on their weaknesses with the intention of addressing them, so that they do not hamper the person's striving towards their development-based objectives. There is nothing wrong about this tactic in DF-CEBC so long as you also help the person focus on their strengths and resources. Thus, it is important to instil in one's coachee the importance of searching for strengths and resources that they already have that they can draw upon to use during DF-CEBC. In particular, it is useful for your coachee to see that the strengths and resources that they have in one area of their life can be applied to other areas.

In addition, it is important to help your coachee to identify and make use of the strengths and resources that others in their environment have that can help them as they work towards their objectives. They can also use their strengths and resources to help others develop themselves as required.

9.1.21. Values

Basically, values are judgements of what your coachee regards as being of vital importance in their life. While values should, ideally, determine your coachee's priorities, they may not because of other more immediate preoccupations that your coachee has in life. If such preoccupations can be seen as proximal factors in your coachee's life, values are seen as distal factors. In general, your coachee will have a vague sense of dissatisfaction when they are not acting in accord with their values, but are not violating them, and a more acute sense of something really being wrong in their life when they are violating their values. An important principle of DF-CEBC is that your coachee will be more committed to pursue their objectives if these are underpinned by important values than when they are not. Thus, discovering what your coachee's values are is an important part of this form of coaching.

Having presented and discussed the 21 principles that form a framework for guiding development-focused cognitive-emotive-behavioural coaching (DF-CEBC), I want to stress that they are best seen as guides for you to use in your work with coachees. Different principles will be relevant with different coachees and it is unlikely that they will all be present in your work with a given coachee. However, it is also unlikely that none will be present in your development-focused work with a person. To help you have an overview of these 21 principles which may serve as a handy aide-memoire when you are working with a coachee in DF-CEBC, I have developed a checklist (Table 9.1).

Table 9.1 Checklist for development-focused CEBC

I have helped (or need to help) my coachee to:	$\underline{Y}$ = Yes (done); $\underline{N}$ = No (Not done yet, but need to do to); $\underline{N/A}$ = Not applicable (don't need to do)
Assume personal responsibility	
Develop flexible and non-extreme attitudes	
Think scientifically and be non-utopian in outlook	
Accept themself unconditionally	
Put themself first in an enlightened self-interested way	
Accept others unconditionally	
Develop social interest	
Be self-directed while being mindful of the social context	
Develop tolerance for uncertainty	
Show strong commitment to meaningful objectives	
Take calculated risks	
Develop discomfort tolerance	
Adopt an outlook of long-range hedonism	
Develop resilience	
Accept life unconditionally	
Adopt a process view of life	
Acquire a self-helping philosophy	
Be realistic about the process of coaching	
Develop a problem-solving mindset	
Identify and use existing strengths and resources in themself and others	
Identify and base coaching on their values	
Principle suggested by your coachee	
Principle suggested by your coachee	

In addition, given that this book presents a pluralistic approach to CEBC, it is important that you discover which principles your coachee thinks it is important to consider in promoting their development and make use of these during coaching. These can also be included in Table 9.1.

9.2. A framework for implementing DF-CEBC

In this part of the chapter, I will discuss a framework for implementing development-focused cognitive-emotive-behavioural coaching. In doing so, I want to underscore the flexible approach being advocated here in that effective DF-CEBC is a fusion between what you, as coach, bring to the process with your professional coaching expertise and what your coachee brings to the process with their personal experience and their own idea about what will be most helpful to them as they strive towards achieving their development-based objectives.

In Chapter 4, I discussed how to respond when the person who is now your coachee has sought your help. In that chapter I discussed how to assess what that person is looking for and how to contract with them on that basis. In the rest of this chapter, I will assume that you have welcomed the person, assessed that they are best suited to development-focused cognitive-emotive-behavioural coaching (DF-CEBC) and have contracted to meet on that basis.

9.2.1. Negotiating a way forward

As you will now have appreciated, the approach to CEBC that is being presented in this book is heavily influenced by the concepts of flexibility and pluralism and the pioneering work done on the coaching alliance pioneered by Ed Bordin (1979). Given that, I suggest that you begin by negotiating with your coachee how best to carry out your mutual tasks in DF-CEBC. My own practice is to outline a proposed way forward and elicit my coachee's responses to this proposal and their own ideas about how DF-CEBC should ideally progress. Then we can refer any differences that we have to the reflection process before agreeing a way forward. Here is a capsule summary of the topics I cover in my proposed way forward. I suggest that:

- My coachee tells me about their development as a person up to this point in their life. I point out that this will help me to understand them in a broad context. This is something that I tend not to do in problem-focused CEBC, as this form of coaching is more focused on problem-solving.
- During this process, I help them to get the most out of the DF-CEBC process by identifying:
  - The personal strengths that they can bring to this process that will enhance it
  - Resources that they can draw on that will help them enhance the process
  - People who can support them though the process
  - Important principles and values that may guide the process.
- They then tell me what they want to achieve from DF-CEBC.
- We prioritise these objectives and focus on one objective at a time.
- I help them to design and carry out action plans to meet their objectives.
- We anticipate and deal with any bumps in the road.
- Once these objectives are met, I encourage my coachee to maintain, enhance and generalise their gains.
- As far as is practicable, I help them to be their own coach.

9.2.2. Giving your coachee an opportunity to tell you about their development as a person

Part of your contract with your coachee in development-focused CEBC concerns how much time the person can spend with you in coaching. If they are being funded for time-limited DF-CEBC or are funding themself for the same, then you need to focus quickly on their objectives (Dryden, 2017). However, if they are funding themself or are being funded for ongoing DF-CEBC, then you have the opportunity to learn a lot about your coachee and how they have developed as a person so that you can base DF-CEBC on such detailed knowledge.

I normally begin such a process by asking my coachee to tell me about themself and their development in whichever way they think will help me to understand them best so I can help them get the most out of the coaching process.

9.2.2.1. The importance of purposeful active listening with prompting

In this section, I will outline my own practice, which I present as an approach to stimulate your own thinking about how to facilitate your coachee's narrative here rather than as an approach to emulate. When a coachee begins to tell their story, my practice is to encourage them to talk in their own way, but I am guided by a number of issues that I want to find out about during this process. I refer to my coaching stance at this point as one that involves active listening, that is purposeful and that involves me prompting the person at various points. The issues that I have in mind that I want to find out about include:

- What parental messages about what is important in life did the person receive and how did they respond to these messages? Which messages did they accept and which did they reject?
- What values were stressed in their upbringing? Who were good role models in this respect and in what way?
- What do they regard as their strengths and weaknesses as a person and have these changed over time?

There are also a number of online resources that you can suggest to your coachee to identify their strengths. One online resource that I suggest is the VIA Institute of Character Survey, where your coachee can take a self-administered test at the end of which they receive a report which outlines their strengths in rank order (24 strengths are listed under the umbrella of six core virtues).[1] Ask them to give you a copy of the report. If you are going to suggest that your coachee takes this test, I recommend that you take it first for yourself so that you can judge for yourself its validity and usefulness.

122 CEBC for development (DF-CEBC)

- What are their interpersonal preferences? Do they like to be in large groups of people, with small groups of people, with a single person or on their own?
- What is their orientation towards interpersonal support? Do they rely on it, accept it when they need it or reject it whether they need it or not?
- How good are they at finding out information they need to obtain? Are they good at discovering and using environmental and interpersonal resources?
- What principles guide them in their lives? For example, my mother used to say: "Son, if you don't ask you don't get." I modified this in later life to: "If you don't ask you don't get, but asking does not guarantee getting."

9.2.3. Helping your coachee to set meaningful objectives

The core of DF-CEBC is to help your coachee to develop themself in whichever life areas they nominate. The more areas they nominate, the longer DF-CEBC will need to be and therefore it is important that you frame your discussions with your coachee concerning this issue with due regard to the length of coaching they have contracted for. Sometimes your coachee will only contract with you for between one and three sessions of DF-CEBC and, if this is the case, I refer you to the book I wrote on the subject (Dryden, 2017).

When you have contracted for ongoing DF-CEBC with your coachee, it is useful to ask them to prepare for a discussion of what they want to get out of this approach to coaching by asking them to complete a form which focuses their attention on this question. I sometimes use the Corrie Inspiration Inventory for this purpose, which is reproduced in Appendix 2. While the form is mainly used in development-focused coaching, the coachee's responses sometimes reveal the existence of an emotional problem that may need to be tackled first. If so, you may need to contract with your coachee for emotional problem-focused CEBC (EPF-CEBC) before working with them to identify their development-based objectives once their emotional problem has effectively addressed.

9.2.3.1. The features of a well-chosen development-based objective

When discussing a development-based objective with your coachee, it is important to bear in mind that a "good" objective in DF-CEBC has the following features:

- It has a direction
- It may be ongoing (thus it may not have an end point)
- When it does have an end point, this point needs to be maintained
- A development-based objective is broad with specific referents.

9.2.3.2. Conditions that facilitate the pursuit of a development-based objective

While setting a development-based objective with your coachee, you should be mindful of the following conditions that facilitate the persistent pursuit of this objective. Thus, an agreed development-based objective should ideally:

- Have intrinsic rather than extrinsic importance. It needs to be important to your coachee rather than only to a stakeholder (e.g. your coachee's employer). When it has both intrinsic and extrinsic importance then these are powerful facilitative conditions.
- Be underpinned by values that are important to your coachee. There are a number of online resources that you can suggest to your coachee to identify their values. One online resource that I suggest is the Personal Values Assessment (PVA) listed on the Barrett Value Centre website, where your coachee can take a self-administered test at the end of which they receive a report which outlines their values. Ask them to give you a copy of the report. As with the VIA Institute of Character Survey, if you are going to suggest that your coachee takes the PVA test, I recommend that you take it first for yourself so that you judge for yourself its validity and usefulness.
- Involve tasks that have intrinsic merit for your coachee.
- Be an objective that your coachee is prepared to integrate into their life. This means:
  - They can devote time to pursuing it on a regular basis
  - They have ready access to any resources they need to pursue the objective
  - It is not going to clash with other priorities that they have in their life.
- Involve active rather than passive desires. It is important to help your coachee to see the distinction between an active desire and a passive desire. Explain to your coachee that an active desire involves something that they want and are prepared to take action to achieve, while a passive desire involves something that your coachee wants but are not willing to take action to achieve. Thus, I am bald and while it would be nice to have hair, I am not going to pursue this option actively, nor am I prepared to bear the considerable expense that taking such action would involve. My desire therefore is passive. If I were prepared to pursue the option of getting hair (e.g. through hair transplants) and bear the cost, then my desire would be active.
- Be an objective for which your coachee is prepared to make sacrifices to achieve.

9.2.4. Helping your coachee to design and implement an action plan

Once you and your coachee have agreed on a development-based objective, the next stage in development-focused CEBC is to help them to devise an action plan and to implement it. In doing so I will also discuss how to help your coachee to anticipate and deal with obstacles to doing both. In brief, devising a plan involves helping your coachee to determine *what* they are going to do to achieve their development-based objective, and implementing the plan involves helping your coachee to determine *how* they are going to put their action plan into practice.

9.2.4.1. Devising the action plan

When helping your coachee to devise an action plan with respect to reaching their developmental-based objective it is important to take the following steps, the order of which is to be determined between the two of you.

9.2.4.1.1 HELP YOUR COACHEE TO DISCOVER CLEAR BENCHMARKS FOR THEIR DEVELOPMENT-BASED OBJECTIVE

While a development-based objective may be broad, it is important that they have specific referents. This is to help your coachee not only to know when they have achieved the objective, if relevant, but also to have clear ideas concerning their progress towards the objective.

Once your coachee has achieved their objective then it is important to ask them how they will know if they are maintaining it. This involves setting clear maintenance benchmarks.

9.2.4.1.2. HELP YOUR COACHEE TO LIST THE ACTIONS THAT THEY NEED TO TAKE TO ACHIEVE THE OBJECTIVE

Once you have helped your coachee to map out a timeline for achieving their objective, the next step is to help them to specify what actions they need to take to meet it. In doing so, it is important to help them select actions that they already have the skills to perform. If they lack a skill that they need, decide with them how they are going to learn it and from whom. On this point, it is important for you to realise that as a coach it is not your job to teach skills that you don't have in your skills repertoire. However, it is your job to help the coachee to find the right resource in this respect. If you can teach a relevant skill to your coachee, do so.

9.2.4.1.3. HELP YOUR COACHEE TO PREPARE A REALISTIC TIME SCHEDULE TO ACHIEVE THEIR OBJECTIVE

This schedule will be determined partly based on the length of your coaching contract with your coachee and how many objectives they wish to set and work towards during the coaching process. Once your coachee has determined the time schedule, help them to allocate tasks to time slots so that you both know what they are planning to do by when. This will need to be monitored and modified on the basis of your coachee's actual experience of implementing the action plan.

9.2.4.1.4. HELP YOUR COACHEE TO USE THEIR STRENGTHS AND OTHER HELPING RESOURCES

When helping your coachee devise an action plan, encourage them to use their strengths and other resources that you helped them to identify earlier.

9.2.4.1.5. ENSURE THAT YOUR COACHEE CAN INTEGRATE THE ACTION PLAN INTO THEIR LIFE

When your coachee integrates their plan into their life it means that they commit themself to act at particular times that are convenient to them and in contexts that are also convenient. If this is not the case, help them to make modifications so that their action plan fits into their life.

9.2.4.1.6. HELP YOUR COACHEE TO IDENTIFY IN ADVANCE POSSIBLE OBSTACLES THAT MAY OCCUR DURING THE PROCESS OF WORKING TOWARDS THE OBJECTIVE

There are three types of potential obstacles that your coachee might identify: i) practical problem obstacles, for which you can use the PRACTICE framework; ii) emotional problem obstacles, for which you can use the Situational ABCDEFG framework; and iii) procrastination. Procrastination-based obstacles may be either practical or emotional in nature or a combination of the two and need careful assessment. I will deal with the issue of obstacles more fully in Chapter 11.

9.2.4.1.7. SUGGEST A LAUNCH DATE AND DECIDE WHETHER TO INFORM OTHERS

You might suggest to your coachee that they may wish to set a launch date for implementing their action plan and, if this resonates with the person, you can discuss what this might involve and if they want to "go public" with this. If this does not appeal to your coachee, have them begin as they wish.

9.2.4.1.8. DEVELOP WITH YOUR COACHEE A WAY OF MONITORING THEIR PROGRESS TO THEIR OBJECTIVE

One of the features of a cognitive-emotive-behavioural approach to coaching is the emphasis it places on collecting data. This is best done by suggesting to your coachee that they keep an action plan diary. This would include information on what they plan to do every day in working towards their objective, what they actually did and their comments on any differences. However, as elsewhere, it is important to elicit and incorporate your coachee's ideas on data collection in your joint decision on the matter.

9.2.4.2. Implementing the action plan

When your coachee has launched their action plan, you have several tasks to perform to help them to stay on course towards their development-based objective.

9.2.4.2.1. MONITOR THE IMPLEMENTATION OF YOUR COACHEE'S ACTION PLAN

Coachees vary a lot on how closely they want their coach to monitor the implementation of their action plans, and this issue should be discussed and decided upon before the action plan is implemented. I will assume here that your coachee does want you to monitor their progress regularly.

Although your coachee will have assigned tasks to time slots (see above), it is important that you are both clear what they are going to do at every point in the implementation stage. This time-action schedule is not one that is set in stone and will need to be changed in light of your coachee's experiences. Consequently, it is important that you monitor their progress on this. Such monitoring involves you both being clear about what your coachee is going to do and reviewing what they did, exploring the meaning of any discrepancies between plans and achievements.

Any changes to your coachee's action plan should emerge out of their experiences of implementing it and any difficulties should be addressed.

9.2.4.2.2. UNDERSTANDING AND DEALING WITH ACTUAL OBSTACLES TO COACHEE PROGRESS

I will deal with this issue fully in Chapter 11. You may want to consult this chapter before reading the case in Chapter 10.

9.2.4.2.3. HELPING YOUR COACHEE TO CAPITALISE ON SUCCESS

When it is clear that your coachee is doing well with respect to their action plan, it is important for you to help them to capitalise on their success. One way of doing this is to find out what it is that they have been doing that has brought about their progress and to suggest that they continue to do what is working for them (Iveson, George & Ratner, 2012). Another way is to encourage them to think of ways that they can generalise what they have been learning from implementing their development-based objective to other relevant areas of their life where they would like to develop themself.

9.2.4.2.4. HELPING YOUR COACHEE TO MAINTAIN THEIR GAINS ONCE THEY HAVE MET THEIR OBJECTIVE

Once your coachee has achieved their objective, it is probable that they will have to take action to maintain the gains that they have met. Thus, it is important that you work with your coachee on the following issues:

- Help them to identify and implement steps they need to take to maintain their gains
- Help them to identify and deal with any obstacles that might interfere with such maintenance strategies
- Help them to develop a high tolerance for discomfort and boredom that they might experience during the maintenance process
- Help them identify and deal with any vulnerability factors that, if encountered, might lead them to experience lapses in the use of their maintenance strategies which, in turn may result in the loss of gains already achieved from DF-CEBC.

9.2.5. Helping your coachee to pursue other objectives and generalise learning

Once your coachee has shown evidence of maintaining their target development-based objective, they are ready to pursue another objective, and you can help them go through the same process with the new objective informed by the work that they have done on the first objective. As they make progress on the second objective, you can encourage them to look for patterns amongst the objectives that they have nominated at the outset and to use these patterns as they increasingly take on the role of their own coach. This also applies to patterns in dealing with obstacles to reaching these objectives to help them to do this you can use such as prompts as:

- What can you learn from dealing with your procrastination on your first objective to help you to prevent you from procrastinating on your other objectives?
- Is there anything from the way you dealt with your anxiety about asserting yourself with your boss that you can use with the prospect of being criticised by your father-in-law?

The more you help your coachee to identify and use helpful patterns of thinking and acting from the work you have done with them on their objectives and dealing effectively with obstacles to reaching these objectives, the more you can help them to formalise these as self-development principles and generalise them across different life domains.

In the following chapter, I will present a case showing DF-CEBC in action in which I will discuss and demonstrate how the issues presented in this chapter were implemented within the context of a particular coaching relationship.

Note

1 The following lists the six core virtues (in italics) with the 24 strengths grouped within the relevant core virtue: *Courage* (bravery, honesty, perseverance, zest); *Humanity* (kindness, love, social intelligence); *Justice* (fairness, leadership, teamwork); *Temperance* (curiosity, forgiveness, humility, prudence, self-regulation); *Transcendence* (appreciation of beauty, gratitude, hope, humour, spirituality); *Wisdom* (creativity, curiosity, judgement, love of learning).

Chapter 10

Kirsten: an example of development-focused cognitive-emotive-behavioural coaching (DF-CEBC)

In this chapter, I will discuss the case of Kirsten, a 36-year-old, single, investment broker. Kirsten was doing well at her firm, but thought that she was not utilising her potential at work. She was also aware that she wasn't getting as much from her personal life as she wanted, and long term she wanted to be married and have a family. At present, she was dating casually, but there was nobody special in her life.

10.1. The brief real-time initial screening conversation with Kirsten

Kirsten was recommended to me by a friend of hers who I had coached in the previous year. At the brief 10-minute phone conversation that I had with Kirsten, I discovered the following:

- Kirsten wanted to develop herself in two areas of her life: work and personal
- She claimed to have no problems to deal with in coaching, whether of a practical nature or of an emotional nature
- Her employer said that they would meet half the costs of her coaching and, on that basis, they would co-fund 20 sessions of coaching
- My fee was within the budget provided by her employer and by herself.

From what Kirsten told me, I said to her that I thought she was a good candidate for development-focused CEBC (DF-CEBC) and that we should meet for a face-to-face session to see if this was the case and to make a contract if we decided to work with one another. Kirsten agreed.

10.2. Assessing Kirsten for CEBC and contracting with her

When I assessed Kirsten's request for coaching in greater depth, she confirmed the information that she gave me on the phone. She was looking to develop herself in two major areas of her life and had no discernible practical or emotional problems that she wanted help with. Thus, it was clear that Kirsten was a good candidate for development-focused coaching. When I explained to her about CEBC, she thought that it could be helpful to her. I then negotiated a contract with Kirsten with respect to confidentiality (it was clear that Kirsten's employer did not want any contact with me unless we both thought that would be helpful), the time-limited nature of coaching (20 sessions), fees and how they would be paid (I would invoice half my fee to Kirsten and half to her employer), my cancellation and referral policies and our respective roles and responsibilities.

10.3. Negotiating a way forward with Kirsten

In the previous chapter, I explored the importance of discussing and negotiating a way forward for coachees in development-focused CEBC. Based on this, Kirsten and I decided to go forward as follows:

- Kirsten did not think that there was much to be gained by her telling me about her development as a person up to this point in their life
- She did think that it was useful for us to begin coaching by identifying:
  - Those personal strengths that she could bring to this process that would enhance it
  - Resources that she could draw on that would help her enhance the process
  - People who could support her though the process
- Kirsten would tell me what she wanted to achieve from DF-CEBC
- We would prioritise these objectives and focus on one objective at a time
- I would help her to design and carry out action plans to meet her objectives
- We would anticipate and deal with any potential obstacles
- Once these objectives were met, and if we had time, I would encourage Kirsten to maintain, enhance and generalise her gains
- She was not interested in me helping her to become her own coach.

10.4. Identifying Kirsten's strengths and resources

As discussed in Chapter 9, in development-focused coaching, it is particularly important to identify those strengths and resources that your coachee has that they can draw upon to get the most out of coaching. I regard these strengths and resources as the foundations of DF-CEBC.

10.4.1. Kirsten's strengths

Here, strengths are defined as "the internal attributes or personality traits and characteristics that can help your coachee to get the most out of development-focused CEBC". I asked Kirsten what strengths she had that would help her to get the most out of coaching. She said that her two most relevant strengths were persistence and open-mindedness. I also asked her whether there would be added value from her taking the online VIA Institute of Character Survey mentioned in Chapter 9, but she did not think so.

10.4.2. Kirsten's resources

Here, resources are defined as "the practical tools or people present in your coachee's life that are available to assist in coaching". Kirsten regarded herself as very proficient at finding out information and resources on the internet and she had built up a network of female colleagues in the wider world of investment banking that she could call upon for help and support. In her personal life, Kirsten remarked that things were somewhat different as virtually all her friends were single. She was surprised when I asked her how many of the women in her work support system were married: she realised that she did not know as they rarely discussed personal issues. My question prompted her to think that she could use the same network as a potential resource when we came to set and pursue objectives in her personal life, particularly as she thought that the women in her work-support network were likely to have faced similar issues concerning how to marry one's work life with one's personal life.

10.5. Identifying useful principles to guide Kirsten's coaching

In Chapter 9, I discussed several principles that can help to guide development-focused CEBC. These can be used in a few ways, including providing them in list form with brief descriptions and having your coachee tell you which principles may help to guide their coaching. At the outset, I offered Kirsten the opportunity to review this list and we decided to do this before I helped her to select her development-based objectives. This can also be done after you have identified your coachee's objectives.

Kirsten identified the following principles that might be useful in guiding her coaching, together with the reasons for her choice. A full description of these principles can be found in Chapter 9.

10.5.1. Enlightened self-interest

Kirsten considered that the principle of enlightened self-interest could be valuable to her, especially in the personal area of her life. She recognised that she had been putting the agenda of her employer and that of several of her family members above that of her own. Particularly with her family members she recognised that she was vulnerable to the self-accusation of being selfish if she put her own agenda ahead of her family. She also realised that this idea was holding her back and needed to be examined.

10.5.2. Uncertainty tolerance

Kirsten recognised that she needed to develop a greater tolerance for uncertainty, particularly at work. In the past, in her view, she made less than optimal investment decisions due to her need to have certainty. In addition, she ended what could have been promising relationships with men because she was not sure what was happening in the relationships.

10.5.3. Calculated risk-taking

Kirsten saw that for her there was a close relationship between taking calculated risks and tolerating uncertainty. She thought that she needed to take more calculated risks in both her work life and her relationships with men.

10.5.4. Long-range hedonism

Kirsten said that she resonated with the concept of long-range hedonism and she said to me that she was prepared to forgo short-term pleasures when these interfered with the pursuit of her long-term development-focused objectives.

10.5.5. Discomfort tolerance

This concept has several features: a) it is hard to tolerate discomfort; b) it is possible to do so; c) tolerate discomfort when it is worth it to you to do so; d) be willing to experience discomfort so that you can tolerate it; and e) make a commitment to tolerate discomfort. Kirsten recognised that she needed to improve her tolerance for discomfort and opined that it would play an important role in coaching.

10.6. Helping Kirsten to set meaningful objectives

As described in Chapter 9, one of my core tasks was to help Kirsten to develop herself in whichever life areas she nominated. She nominated her work and her personal life, and in negotiating her objectives we had to be mindful of the fact that our contract was for 20 sessions. My work in helping Kirsten select sound development-based objectives was guided by the following ideas about what these constitute (see Chapter 9 for a full discussion of these points). They should:

- Have a direction
- Be ongoing (thus it may not have an end point), and when they do have such end points, these need to be maintained
- Be specific, and when they are often broad, these should have specific referents

- Have intrinsic rather than extrinsic importance for the person
- Be underpinned by values that are important to the person
- Involve tasks that have intrinsic merit for the person
- Be capable of being integrated into the person's life
- Involve active rather than passive desires (see Chapter 9)
- Be objectives for which the person is prepared to make sacrifices to achieve.

Based on these points, Kirsten set the following two objectives:

1. *At work*, I want to take more calculated risks, as shown by making purchases and sales that I know could be beneficial that I currently don't make because I am not sure they will work out well
2. *In my personal life*, as I want to get married and have a family, I want to devote more time (at least two hours a day) to meet eligible men.

10.7. Helping Kirsten to design and implement her action plans

Once Kirsten and I agreed on these development-based objectives, the next stage was for us to decide in which order we were going to deal with them. Kirsten suggested that we deal with them both at the same time, devoting half a coaching session to each. I was happy to go along with this suggestion so long as Kirsten agreed to work equally towards both these objectives outside coaching sessions. She agreed to do this.

Then, I helped Kirsten to devise an action plan for both objectives and later to implement them. As advised in Chapter 9, I also helped Kirsten to anticipate and deal with any obstacles that may occur during this part of the coaching process. If you recall, when I help Kirsten devise action plans this involves me encouraging her to determine *what* she is going to do to achieve her development-based objectives, and when I help her to implement these plans I am encouraging her to determine *how* she is going to put these action plans into practice.

10.7.1. Helping Kirsten to devise her action plans

I will deal with Kirsten's action plans for her two development-based objectives separately.

10.7.1.1. Helping Kirsten to devise her action plan with respect to her work-related objective

To be clear about what we were discussing, Kirsten and I created the following scheme. This is a good example of CEBC's focus on specificity.

A = Making purchases and sales when I am sure that I am doing the right thing. Here, I would be taking a small risk.
B = Making purchases and sales when I am unsure, but when it is probably the right thing to do. Here, I would be taking a moderate risk.
C = Making purchases and sales when I am unsure, but when it is probably the wrong thing to do. Here, I would be taking a large risk.
D = Not making purchases and sales when I am sure that I am doing the right thing. Here, I would be taking a small risk.

Devising this scheme helped Kirsten see what she needed to concentrate on. She had no difficulties acting in zones A and D and did not want to act in zone C. She wanted to focus on her behaviour in zone B.

She also realised one very important thing when devising this scheme. In the past, when faced with being unsure about making a purchase or a sale she always saw herself as being in zone C. Thus, she always associated her uncertainty with taking a large risk, which she was not prepared to do. She could now see that faced with being unsure about making a purchase or a sale, she could be in zone B. Thus, uncertainty did involve risk, but she could judge on a case by case basis whether the risk was moderate or large. At this point, Kirsten told me that one negative point that came out of her semi-annual appraisals was that her line manager did not think that she was taking enough calculated risks in buying and selling. She was too conservative in this area of her work. Now being able to differentiate between moderate risk-related uncertainty and large-risk related uncertainty, she could process this feedback more fully and she realised that her company would support her work-related development-based objective.

I asked Kirsten if she needed to consult a professional resource at the same time as seeing me, as I have no knowledge in her field of expertise. In response, Kirsten said that the issue was not knowledge-based but psychology-based. At this point I reminded her that she could bring her strengths of persistence and open-mindedness to this part of the coaching process.

The first stage in developing a work-related action plan was for Kirsten to collect data over a two-week period on her behaviour on this issue. Together we developed a data-collection form (see Table 10.1).

One of the effects of self-monitoring is that it tends to change the behaviour that is being monitored (Korotitsch & Nelson-Gray, 1999). This seemed to happen with Kirsten, who, in the first week of data collection, reported on the following:

- 12 purchase opportunities of moderate risk [zone B] – 6 actual purchases – 50% success rate
- 9 sale opportunities of moderate risk [zone B] – 4 actual sales – 44% success rate.

Table 10.1 Kirsten's data-collection form to assess the risk of investment deals and her subsequent decisions

Date and time	Purchase or sale opportunity	Uncertainty: level of risk ('B' or 'C')	My decision	Comments

B = Making a purchase or sale when I am unsure, but when it is probably the right thing to do. Here, I would be taking a moderate risk.
C = Making a purchase and sale when I am unsure, but when it is probably the wrong thing to do. Here, I would be taking a large risk.

These data, which indicated to Kirsten that she was taking more calculated risks than before self-monitoring based on the differentiation of risk, helped Kirsten to be clearer about two things. First, she wanted to aim for a 90% success rate in zone B in both the purchase and sale categories. Second, while realising that she had hitherto completely associated uncertainty with large risk was important, it was insufficient in helping her to reach her 90% success objective. This meant that Kirsten and I needed to do some work on understanding the potential obstacle(s) to her reaching her objective of a 90% success rate with respect to her behaviour in zone B. We needed to do this work before she implemented her action plan to continue to differentiate between moderate risk-related uncertainty and large risk-related uncertainty and to act on the former 90% of the time, but not on the latter. I will discuss how I helped her deal with this obstacle later in the chapter. But, first, let me show you how I helped her devise an action plan with respect to her objective in her personal life.

10.7.1.2. Helping Kirsten to devise her action plan with respect to her personal life-related objective

You will recall that Kirsten's development-based objective in her personal life was to devote more time (at least two hours a day) to meet eligible men because she wanted to get married and have a family. Normally a development-related objective indicates a person's wish to get the most out of themselves in an area in which they are already functioning adequately or well. This was the case with Kirsten's work-related objective. However, in the nominated life area of "meeting men", Kirsten was presently doing nothing.

She realised that her work had completely dominated her life and that at the age of 36 she needed to do something to change her "work–personal life" balance. While a person's absence of functioning in an area can indicate the presence of an emotional problem manifest by avoidance, for me this had quite a different "feel". I did not get the sense that Kirsten was avoiding meeting men, but that she was so keen to do well in her job that she neglected other areas of her life. Kirsten agreed with this formulation and therefore we treated the issue as one that needed development-focused CEBC (DF-CEBC) rather than emotional problem-focused CEBC (EPF-CEBC). If Kirsten's absence of functioning in this area of her personal life was explained by avoidance, then we would have employed EPF-CEBC. Using a DF-CEBC approach with this issue did not mean that Kirsten had no emotional problems in this area. It only indicated that none were obviously present at our initial assessment of the issue.

Kirsten realised, of course, that as she was making no effort to meet men then she was not progressing with her overall objective of being married with a family. While her workplace was predominantly male oriented, romantic or sexual relationships between work colleagues were frowned upon by her employer, and in any case would have been against Kirsten's values. I helped Kirsten devise the following action plan. She would work towards spending at least two hours every day on activities designed to meet men. These included:

- Online dating activities
- Engaging in social and other activities where there were likely to be eligible men
- Activities related to joining an upmarket dating agency
- Letting friends and women from her support network know that she was interested in meeting eligible men.

Kirsten devised the following plan:

- Week 1: Spending 0.5 hour a day minimum on dating-related activities
- Week 2: Spending 1.0 hour a day minimum on dating-related activities
- Week 3: Spending 1.5 hours a day minimum on dating-related activities
- Week 4 onwards: Spending 2.0 hours a day minimum on dating-related activities.

She thought that this plan was doable and could be integrated into her life.

10.7.2. Helping Kirsten to implement her action plans

Both Kirsten's action plans were easy to implement and required very little input from me. With respect to her work-related action plan, Kirsten identified a potential obstacle that we had to investigate and deal with, if necessary.

10.7.2.1. Understanding and dealing with Kirsten's potential obstacle to meeting her work-related objective

You will recall that Kirsten's work-related objective was for her to take uncertainty-related moderate risks with respect to purchasing and selling investments for her clients 90% of the time.[1] While she found it useful to understand that not all uncertainty-related risk was large, the early data-collection on her existing buying and selling behaviour indicated the possible existence of an obstacle that needed exploring. This is how I helped her to explore and ultimately deal with what turned out to be an actual obstacle.

WINDY: Let's take an instance when you wanted to take a moderate risk, but didn't. Try to choose an example that might be representative of other instances when you failed to take your desired action.

KIRSTEN: Well, an investment purchasing opportunity came up and I had some doubts about it, but I knew enough about the investment to tell me that it would involve me taking a moderate risk rather than a large risk and therefore according to my plan I should have made a purchase, but I did not do so.

WINDY: What is your hypothesis concerning why you didn't?

KIRSTEN: I think that it has something to do with feeling uncomfortable.

WINDY: OK. Shall we go through the five components of discomfort tolerance to see if we can pinpoint the problem?

KIRSTEN: That would be a good idea.

WINDY: OK, so what I want you to do is to imagine that you are back in the situation where you are faced with the choice of purchasing the moderate risk investment or not doing so. Can you imagine that?

KIRSTEN: Yes, I can.

WINDY: Now did you feel discomfort and then decide not to make the purchase or did you decide not to make the purchase because you thought you would feel uncomfortable if you did purchase it?

KIRSTEN: Oh, I remember feeling very uncomfortable and decided not to make the purchase.

WINDY: And when you made that decision, what happened to the discomfort?

KIRSTEN: It went away, but I was immediately cross with myself that I did not make the purchase.

WINDY: Was that feeling of annoyance easier to deal with than the purchase-related discomfort?

KIRSTEN: Very much so. It's less acute and more familiar to me.

[What I am doing here is assessing the adversity to which Kirsten responded with avoidance. This seemed to be the strong level of discomfort she experienced when faced with making the purchase of the moderate risk investment.]

WINDY: So, on a 1–10 scale of discomfort, how strong was your level of discomfort before you chose not to make the purchase?

KIRSTEN: I would say an 8.

WINDY: How much weaker would it have had to have been for you to make the purchase?

KIRSTEN: Interesting question. Let me think ... a 5.

WINDY: Do you think that if your discomfort level is an 8, then the risk you would be taking would be larger than if your discomfort level is a 5?

KIRSTEN: Well, put like that it sounds stupid, but yes.

WINDY: Why is that stupid?

KIRSTEN: Because it's the same situation. I'm saying that the risk is larger because my level of discomfort is greater.

WINDY: So, if you have judged the level of risk as moderate and you find yourself again backing away from purchasing an investment, what can you remind yourself of?

KIRSTEN: That my gut instinct says that the risk is large, but my brain has assessed it as moderate and I am going to act on what my brain tells me not on what my gut tells me.

WINDY: Even if your level of discomfort is a 9?

KIRSTEN: Yes.

WINDY: What if it's a 10?

KIRSTEN: Even then.

WINDY: So, can you tell me what the take-home message is here?

KIRSTEN: That once my brain has assessed a risk as moderate, I tend to increase the size of that risk if my level of discomfort is high. However, while this might be my first response, I can stand back and recognise what is happening and act on my brain's assessment of risk rather than my gut's assessment and I can do this no matter how intense my level of discomfort.

WINDY: That's a great summary. Can I suggest that you write that down?

KIRSTEN: Good idea.

WINDY: Now let's look at what happened from a slightly different perspective. Leaving aside the risk assessment issue and your level of discomfort, if we take that level which you rated as an 8 at the time, would it have been a struggle to tolerate it?

KIRSTEN: Yes.

WINDY: At the time, do you think that you could have tolerated it?

KIRSTEN: Yes, I think I could.

WINDY: Also, did you think it was worth it to you to do so?

KIRSTEN: I believe so, yes.

WINDY: Were you willing to experience the discomfort?

KIRSTEN: No, I guess not.

WINDY: And did you make a commitment to do so?

KIRSTEN: No, I didn't.

WINDY: So, if you were to encounter the same situation again and you were willing to experience the discomfort and committed yourself to doing so

Table 10.2 Kirsten's results in implementing her action plan

Week	Purchase (P) and sales (S) opportunities (moderate risk)	Actual purchases (P) and sales (S)	Percentage
1	P – 11	P – 9	82%
	S – 9	S – 7	78%
2	P – 13	P – 11	85%
	S – 10	S – 8	80%
3	P – 12	P – 11	92%
	S – 10	S – 9	90%

and then you stood back and saw that the risk was still moderate, what would you do?

KIRSTEN: I would purchase the investment even if I felt very uncomfortable.

WINDY: So, what's the additional take-home point here?

KIRSTEN: That I need to be willing to and committed to experience discomfort rather than acting quickly to get rid of it. Shall I make a note?

WINDY: Great idea.

Armed with these two take-home points: 1) Be willing and committed to experience high levels of discomfort, and 2) Act on my brain's assessment of risk and not on my gut's assessment, Kirsten then implemented her action plan. Her first three weeks' results are shown in Table 10.2.

Kirsten applied the learning from her in-session discussion with me about dealing with discomfort (see above) and, as can be seen from the above results, she met her work-related objectives in three weeks.

10.7.2.2. Understanding and dealing with Kirsten's obstacles while implementing her dating-related action plan

As mentioned above, Kirsten needed very little input from me in implementing her dating-related action plan.[2] Where my input was required was when she encountered several issues along the way.

10.7.2.2.1. BEING CLEAR ABOUT HER CRITERIA AND BEING FLEXIBLE

When Kirsten began to implement her action plan, it became clear that she did not have very clear criteria about the kind of man who she was looking for. She held a number of romantic and vague notions like "I will know him when I meet him," "I want a man like my father" and "Being precise in my thinking takes the romance out of dating." She was unresponsive when I asked her to stand back and look at these notions. However, when Kirsten signed up for an expensive up-market introduction agency and they asked her similar questions, she became more responsive to the idea of specifying her criteria. I pointed out that she could do this as well as allow herself to be flexible about these criteria and be guided by her romantic ideas about meeting people. This again demonstrates the flexible and pluralistic approach that underpins CEBC.

10.7.2.2.2. DEALING WITH SHAME ABOUT ASKING WOMEN FROM HER PROFESSIONAL SUPPORT NETWORK TO INTRODUCE HER TO ELIGIBLE MEN

Kirsten was very diligent in implementing her action plan, so when she reported that she had not done something that we had both agreed she would do, this pointed to the existence of an obstacle that needed to be addressed. She had not told women from her professional support network that she was looking to meet someone and thus did not ask them to introduce her to eligible men. She first explained that this was not something that the network is for, but admitted in response to my question how she would react if another woman had reached out to network in this way that she would not have minded at all. After some discussion, it appeared that her reluctance was underpinned by shame. She regarded herself as a weak, incompetent person who absolutely should be able to find a man on her own and not ask for help. Here is how I responded to this idea.

WINDY: So, you would see yourself as a weak person if you have to admit that you need help to find a man from your support network?
KIRSTEN: Yes, I would.
WINDY: If another woman in your network had reached out to the group in the same way, would you look down on her and think, "She is a weak person who should be able to find a man on her own?"
KIRSTEN: No, of course not.
WINDY: Why not?
KIRSTEN: Because she is an ordinary person who is struggling in an area where many women struggle.
WINDY: So, would you support her and introduce her to someone you know with whom she might get on?
KIRSTEN: 100%
WINDY: So, now I'm confused. You would see her as an ordinary woman struggling in a difficult area and you would support and help her. However, when your spotlight is on you, you view yourself as a weak person who should be able to find someone on your own. What's the difference between you and her?
KIRSTEN: I don't know, it just feels I should be able to do it on my own.
WINDY: But does that feeling make it true?
KIRSTEN: I guess not.

WINDY: Can you see the similarity between this and the "feeling" you had that uncertainty about purchasing and selling meant that you were facing a large risk?

KIRSTEN: Yes.

WINDY: And what did you do with that feeling?

KIRSTEN: I questioned the idea behind it.

WINDY: What would happen if you questioned the idea behind the feeling that you are a weak person for not finding a man on your own while other women are not weak and deserve supporting?

KIRSTEN: I would see that I am like other women, ordinary and worthy of support when struggling.

WINDY: And is this true whether or not you have the "feeling" that you are weak?

KIRSTEN: Yes, it is.

WINDY: So, what are you going to act on, what your brain tells you or what your gut tells you?

KIRSTEN: My brain.

WINDY: Even if you might feel uncomfortable doing so?

KIRSTEN: Yes.

WINDY: And even if that discomfort is strong?

KIRSTEN: Yes, I just need to remind myself that I am willing to experience it and committed to act when I feel it.

This is another example of the use of engaging a coachee in a dialectical discussion when they hold an idea or attitude that is counterproductive. Note the similarity of themes that emerged when Kirsten talked about using her "feelings" to judge the veracity and usefulness of an idea in both life areas. This happens often in all forms of CEBC.

After this discussion, Kirsten went to her support network and asked for their help and received a supportive and compassionate response and was given some leads about meeting some eligible men.

10.7.2.2.3. ASKING MEN OUT

Kirsten believed that women "should not" have to ask men out and was very reluctant to take the lead in this area. Consequently, she passed on opportunities to get to know several men she was interested in. I suggested that she poll the women that she knew in both her personal life and in her professional support work and the majority response was that in this day and age it is perfectly acceptable for women to ask men out. Kirsten took this and began to ask men out even though it was her uncomfortable for her to do so. Kirsten was also advised on this and on other dating issues by a dating coach who was provided by the introduction agency she had joined.

10.7.2.2.4. DEALING WITH BEING REJECTED AND REJECTING

Another issue that Kirsten and I discussed, as it appeared to be problematic for her, was rejection. More specifically, we discussed how to take rejection and how to reject someone (Jiang, 2016). From our discussions, Kirsten took away the following points which she acted on.

- Being rejected and rejecting people are almost inevitable when trying to find a partner.[3] Dating is therefore a numbers game.
- Being rejected by someone indicates that the mix is not right for the person rather than that there is something wrong with me. The same goes for when I reject someone.
- If I am rejected many times for the same reason, it does not mean I am worthless. Rather, it means that I am an ordinary person with an issue that needs attention.
- Being rejected is painful, but being with someone who wants to end the relationship with me, but who is too scared to do so, is much worse.
- Rejecting someone is very uncomfortable, but being with someone who I want to break up with to avoid such discomfort is far worse for me and for the other person.
- When I reject someone, I will do so with sensitivity, but I am not responsible for how they take it. If they are very upset, this is not a reason to resume the relationship.
- I will end a relationship in person, wherever possible, but others do not have to do the same.

10.7.2.2.5. DEALING WITH IMPATIENCE

Kirsten mentioned that one of the strengths that she thought would be useful in coaching was persistence. But even this was called into question as she went on one unproductive date after the other. At times, she wanted to end the process, and at these times we found that she was holding the following rigid attitude: "Because I am putting so much into this process, my efforts must be rewarded more quickly than is happening." Kirsten could see how this attitude was leading her to become impatient with progress and made her vulnerable to quitting the process, so I engaged her in a dialectical discussion on this issue and helped her to develop a more flexible attitude towards the speed of the process as follows: "Because I am putting so much into this process, it would be very nice if my efforts were rewarded more quickly than is happening, but sadly it does not have to be the way I want it to be." This flexible attitude helped Kirsten to accept things as they were and to continue to persist for as long as it took to achieve her objective.

The work that I did with Kirsten on the attitudes and thinking that underpinned some of the obstacles she encountered in achieving her objectives was similar to the work that I do in emotional problem-focused CEBC

(EPF-CEBC). As such, it is my considered view that CEBC coaches do need to develop the skills that I discussed in Chapter 7 even if they just focus on development-focused CEBC.

10.7.3. Helping Kirsten to maintain her gains once she met her objectives

Once Kirsten achieved her work-related objective of a 90% success rate on moderate risk-related investments, I monitored this every subsequent week by reviewing her daily log which she continued to keep. After hitting her target, she maintained these, often reporting a 100% success rate.

Kirsten was also able to maintain her two-hour-per-day dating-related activity schedule with a little help from me when she began to become impatient (see above).

Kirsten's success at meeting her work-related objective brought immediate results – her portfolio profits increased and both her clients and her employer were very pleased with the change in her investing behaviour. By contrast, Kirsten experienced a different outcome as a result of meeting her dating-related time objectives. While she met far more men than she had in the previous two years, she was finding it difficult to meet those with whom she would like to develop a relationship who felt the same about her. Interestingly, her expensive high-end introduction agency was no more helpful in this respect than online dating sites!

10.7.4. Ending the DF-CEBC process with Kirsten (see Chapter 12)

If you recall, Kirsten and I had contracted for 20 sessions of coaching, which occurred weekly over the course of 20 weeks. At this final session, we agreed that we would review our coaching and plan for a follow-up review session. However, Kirsten came in quite excited to report that she had had a third date with a man whom the introduction agency had found and that things looked very promising. We discussed this and manged to review our coaching, which for Kirsten had been very successful. At work, clearly, she was able to meet her objectives quite quickly and had maintained these gains to the delight of all concerned (see above). She had devoted time to her personal life, which she had neglected for a number of years, and was steadily working towards finding a partner, updating some ideas along the way which would have been obstacles if we had not discussed and addressed them. She was more sanguine than hitherto that the dating process that she had launched and maintained would bear fruit in the future.

10.7.5. My follow-up session with Kirsten (see Chapter 12)

Kirsten and I agreed to hold a follow-up session three months after the end of coaching to evaluate the outcome of coaching and the service that I provided.

From an outcome perspective, Kirsten had maintained and sometimes surpassed her 90% success rate with the moderate risk-related activities at work and was still going out with the man that she talked about at our final coaching session. Given this, she had suspended her search until, and if, it was necessary to resume it.

From a service evaluation perspective, Kirsten was very complimentary about our coaching and about my input as a coach, particularly mentioning how I helped her to question some of the ideas and attitudes she had towards risk and dating. Both she and her employer thought that they had enjoyed a good return on their respective investment in Kirsten's coaching, which coming from investment brokers was praise indeed![4]

In the next chapter, I will consider how to deal with obstacles in CEBC. I have alluded to this issue at several points in the book, but it now warrants more focused discussion.

Notes

1 I suggest that you read Chapter 11 if you want a fuller picture about how to deal with obstacles in coaching before reading the material in this section.
2 Again, I suggest that you read Chapter 11 if you want a fuller picture about how to deal with obstacles in coaching before reading the material in this section.
3 Some people do marry the first person they ever meet, but this is rare these days.
4 About a year after follow-up, I received news that Kirsten had got engaged to the man she had been going out with.

Chapter 11
Identifying, understanding and dealing with obstacles in CEBC

An obstacle in CEBC is something that blocks the coachee's path towards their development-based objective in DF-CEBC or their problem-based goal in PF-CEBC[1] or something that hinders their progress towards this objective or goal. In this chapter I will focus mainly on obstacles to which the coachee responds in an unhealthy way, emotionally, behaviourally and cognitively. The goal of helping the coachee in CEBC is to help them deal with the obstacle so that it is not in fact an obstacle, in that the coachee can return to the business of pursuing their objective in DF-CEBC or their goal in PF-CEBC. Since the issues in dealing with such obstacles are essentially the same in both forms of CEBC, they can be dealt with in one chapter. Also, anything that I say here about identifying, understanding and dealing with actual obstacles can also be applied to helping the coachee anticipate, understand and deal with potential obstacles.

11.1. Identify the type of obstacle the coachee is facing

There are four types of obstacle that the coachee might encounter:

- *An external adversity occurs that is related to the CEBC process (e.g. someone criticises the coachee as they put into practice their coaching plan).* Here, the coach can help the coachee address the obstacle using either the "PRACTICE" problem-solving framework if the coachee's obstacle is indicative of a practical problem or the "Situational ABCDEFG" framework if it is indicative of an emotional problem.
- *An external adversity occurs that is not related to the CEBC process (e.g. one of coachee's relatives is very ill).* If the coachee has an emotional problem about this, then the coach can help by using the "Situational ABCDEFG" framework. If the obstacle leads to a practical problem, then the "PRACTICE" framework can be employed. However, it may be that while the coachee has neither a practical nor an emotional problem about this adversity, its presence may mean that the coachee has neither

the time nor the focus to continue in coaching for the time being and a break from coaching may be indicated. Here the coach invites the coachee to resume the process when the person has both the time and the mental space to devote to pursuing their coaching objectives.
- *An internal adversity occurs that is related to the CEBC process (e.g. the coachee begins to avoid doing tasks that they need to carry out to achieve their objective/goal, and there is no external reason for this avoidance).* This is usually indicative of an emotional problem, which can be dealt with by the coach using the "Situational ABCDEFG" framework. However, if it transpires that this is due to a practical problem, then the "PRACTICE" framework can be employed.
- *The coachee encounters an environmental change which threatens the continuation of the CEBC process (e.g. the coachee has taken on a lot more work to cover for a sick colleague).* Here the coach helps the coachee use the PRACTICE framework to determine whether they can find a way of dealing with the environmental change. If not, this may mean that the coachee postpones coaching, particularly if they are pursuing a development-based objective, until they have the time to devote to it.

11.2. Decide what to do with the obstacle

Once the coach has identified what type of obstacle the coachee has encountered, their next step is to decide with the coachee what to do with it. Here are the available options and when they might decide to implement them, in conjunction with the coachee.

11.2.1. Deal with the obstacle in CEBC

Here, the coach and coachee decide to deal with the obstacle within CEBC because they both think that the coach can help the coachee deal with it. Once this is done then the coachee can resume the pursuit of their development-based objective or problem-related goal.

11.2.2. Agree that the coachee will deal with the obstacle on their own

Occasionally it happens that when the coachee discovers the nature of the obstacle that is interfering with their pursuit towards their objective/goal, they realise that they already have the resources to deal with the obstacle on their own. The coach's assessment of the type of obstacle that they were facing helped them to understand the obstacle, and now they have this understanding they are confident that they can deal with it independently of the coach's offer to help them deal with it within CEBC. In which case, the coach should allow them to deal with the obstacle on their own and only offer assistance if it becomes clear that the obstacle is still present despite the coachee's attempts to address it.

11.2.3. The coachee chooses not respond to the obstacle

When your computer's virus protection system detects a virus, it places it in a vault. This means that the virus is still present, but does not have any impact on the operation of your computer. It is "walled off". Sometimes when the coach helps the coachee to identify the type of obstacle that is having a negative impact on the progress that they are making towards their development-based objective or problem-based goal, they think that they can "wall it off" now that they know what it is, and consequently they think they can resume their work towards their objective. This is particularly the case when the adversity is an external one that is not related to the CEBC process. When the coachee uses this "walling off" strategy, the coach will soon learn if it is successful or not. The time for the coach to intervene is when their "walling off" strategy has proven unsuccessful.

11.3. How to deal with the obstacle

When the coach and coachee decide to work on the obstacle in CEBC, then their first priority is to identify the obstacle and to decide whether it is indicative of a practical problem or an emotional problem. If it indicates a practical problem, then the "PRACTICE" framework of practical problem-solving can be used (see Chapters 5–6), while if it indicates an emotional problem, then the "Situational ABCDEFG" framework of emotional problem-solving can be used (see Chapters 7–8).

11.3.1. How to deal with an emotional problem about an emotional problem

One common obstacle that is worthy of mention here is when the person has an emotional problem about their original emotional problem, and the presence of this "meta-emotional" problem[2] means that the person cannot focus sufficiently on their "primary" emotional problem. When this occurs the CEBC coach helps the coachee in the following way:

- Agree with the coachee to focus on the meta-emotional problem
- Assess a specific example of the meta-emotional problem, using the "Situational ABCDEFG" framework
- Focus on the problematic emotional, behavioural and cognitive responses at "C". Shame is a common meta-emotional problem, for example
- Identify the "A". Discover what the coachee found particularly disturbing about the primary emotional problem. This could be the feelings or

sensations the person experienced or the meaning of the problem for the coachee (e.g. "Having this problem is evidence that I have a weakness")
- Identify the coachee's goal. Encourage them to strive towards healthy ways of responding to the original emotional problem
- Identify the rigid/extreme attitudes the person held towards their original emotional problem and their alternative flexible/non-extreme attitudes
- Engage the coachee in a dialectical examination of both sets of attitudes
- Encourage the coachee to rehearse and act in ways that are consistent with their developing flexible and non-extreme attitudes towards their original emotional problem until they are ready to return to dealing with it free from the obstructing effects of the meta-emotional problem.

In the final chapter, I will discuss how the coach can suitably bring the CEBC process to an end, and some of the issues concerning follow-up and evaluation.

Notes

1 When I discuss PF-CEBC in this chapter, I refer to both practical problem-focused CEBC and emotional problem-focused CEBC, unless otherwise specified.
2 The term "meta-emotional problem" means having an emotional problem about an emotional problem.

Chapter 12

Ending and follow-up

In this final chapter, I will discuss how CEB coaches tend to work towards ending the CEBC process with their coachees. I will also discuss the issue of follow-up and the evaluation of CEBC.

12.1. Ending the CEBC process

Once a coachee has made progress in achieving and maintaining some or most of their development-based objectives and problem-based goals, shown evidence that they can generalise their learning to other life areas and can, in some important ways, carry on the coaching process for themselves, then it may be time to discuss how the coachee and coach are going to end the process. Of course, the ending may have already been specified at the outset in the coaching contract the coach made with their coachee, but if this is not the case, it does need to be discussed, preferably well before the formal end of the process. Often the CEB coach and coachee agree to meet less often as the latter makes progress towards their objectives and wishes to become more autonomous in the process. Thus, there is no one correct way to end CEB coaching. Rather, the ending needs to be a "good one", and that is most likely to occur when it has been fully discussed and agreed between the coach and coachee.

At the final session, it is important for the coach to give the coachee an opportunity to summarise what has gone well in the process and what they learned from it. The coach's role here is basically a listening and clarifying one and perhaps to prompt the coachee to focus on any areas not covered by their summary and learning statement. It is also important for the coach to give the coachee an opportunity to raise any matters of unfinished business and to help the coachee gain closure. It is important to seek feedback from the coachee concerning what was valuable about the process and what was not helpful, if these issues have not been covered by the coachee's summary and learning statement.

Finally, the coach should discuss with the coachee the issues of follow-up and evaluation.

12.2. Follow-up

CEB coaches conduct a follow-session for the following reasons:

1. Follow-up provides an opportunity for the coachee to give feedback on what they have done in the time between the last time they saw their coach and the follow-up session.
2. Knowing that there is a feedback session scheduled offers the coachee a sense of care and connection with their coach.
3. A follow-up session provides the coachee with an opportunity to request more coaching help if needed, whether this is development-focused or problem-focused.
4. Follow-up enables the coach and any organisation in which the coach works to carry out outcome evaluation (i.e. how your coachee has done). If the coach does this, then they will have to give some thought to how they are going to measure outcome and what forms, if any, they are going to use.
5. Follow-up provides service evaluation data (what the coachee thought of the help provided) and such data will help the coach and any organisation in which they work to improve the service offered.

My own practice is to conduct the follow-up session three months after coaching has ended, but this will vary according to the coach, the service in which they work, if relevant, and the coachee.

12.3. Evaluation

The subject of evaluating coaching is a complex one and one that lies outside the scope of this book. For an extended discussion of the issues concerning coaching evaluation, I refer you to Gray (2004) and Carter (2006). Having said that, my own approach to outcome evaluation is to construct an individualised measure with my coachee to provide pre- and post-coaching data with respect to their development-based objectives or problem-based goals and which also allows us to monitor the coachee's progress towards achieving these objectives or goals.

Appendix 1

A guide to the eight emotional problems and their healthy alternatives with adversities, basic attitudes and associated behaviour and thinking

Anxiety vs. concern

Adversity	You are facing a threat to your personal domain	
Basic attitude	**RIGID AND EXTREME**	**FLEXIBLE AND NON-EXTREME**
Emotion	Anxiety	Concern
Behaviour	• You avoid the threat • You withdraw physically from the threat • You ward off the threat (e.g. by rituals or superstitious behaviour) • You try to neutralise the threat (e.g. by being nice to people of whom you are afraid) • You distract yourself from the threat by engaging in other activity • You keep checking on the current status of the threat hoping to find that it has disappeared or become benign • You seek reassurance from others that the threat is benign • You seek support from others so that if the threat happens they will handle it or be there to rescue you • You over-prepare in order to minimise the threat happening or so that you are prepared to meet it (NB it is the over-preparation that is the problem here) • You tranquillise your feelings so that you don't think about the threat • You overcompensate for feeling vulnerable by seeking out an even greater threat to prove to yourself that you can cope	• You face up to the threat without using any safety-seeking measures • You take constructive action to deal with the threat • You seek support from others to help you face up to the threat and then take constructive action by yourself rather than rely on them to handle it for you or to be there to rescue you • You prepare to meet the threat but do not over-prepare

Subsequent thinking	Threat-exaggerated thinking • You overestimate the probability of the threat occurring • You underestimate your ability to cope with the threat • You ruminate about the threat • You create an even more negative threat in your mind • You magnify the negative consequences of the threat and minimise its positive consequences • You have more task-irrelevant thoughts than in "concern" Safety-seeking thinking • You withdraw mentally from the threat • You try to persuade yourself that the threat is not imminent and that you are imagining it • You think in ways designed to reassure yourself that the threat is benign or, if not, that its consequences will be insignificant • You distract yourself from the threat, e.g. by focusing on mental scenes of safety and well-being • You over-prepare mentally in order to minimise the threat happening or so that you are prepared to meet it (NB once again it is the over-preparation that is the problem here) • You picture yourself dealing with the threat in a masterful way • You overcompensate for your feeling of vulnerability by picturing yourself dealing effectively with an even bigger threat	• You are realistic about the probability of the threat occurring • You view the threat realistically • You realistically appraise your ability to cope with the threat • You think about what to do concerning dealing with threat constructively rather than ruminate about the threat • You have more task-relevant thoughts than in "anxiety" • You picture yourself dealing with the threat in a realistic way

Depression vs. sadness

Adversity	• You have experienced a loss from the sociotropic and/or autonomous realms of your personal domain • You have experienced failure within the sociotropic and/or autonomous realms of your personal domain • You or others have experienced an undeserved plight	
Basic attitude	**RIGID AND EXTREME**	**FLEXIBLE AND NON-EXTREME**
Emotion	Depression	Sadness
Behaviour	• You become overly dependent on and seek to cling to others (particularly in sociotropic depression) • You bemoan your fate or that of others to anyone who will listen (particularly in pity-based depression) • You create an environment consistent with your depressed feelings • You attempt to terminate feelings of depression in self-destructive ways • You either push away attempts to comfort you (in autonomous depression) or use such comfort to reinforce your dependency (in sociotropic depression) or your self- or other-pity (in pity-based depression)	• You seek out reinforcements after a period of mourning (particularly when your inferential theme is loss) • You create an environment inconsistent with depressed feelings • You express your feelings about the loss, failure or undeserved plight and talk in a non-complaining way about these feelings to significant others • You allow yourself to be comforted in a way that helps you to express your feelings of sadness and mourn your loss
Subsequent thinking	• You see only negative aspects of the loss, failure or undeserved plight • You think of other losses, failures and undeserved plights that you (and in the case of the latter, others) have experienced • You think you are unable to help yourself (helplessness) • You only see pain and blackness in the future (hopelessness) • You see yourself being totally dependent on others (in autonomous depression) • You see yourself as being disconnected from others (in sociotropic depression) • You see the world as full of undeservedness and unfairness (in plight-based depression) • You tend to ruminate concerning the source of your depression and its consequences	• You are able to recognise both negative and positive aspects of the loss or failure • You think you are able to help yourself • You look to the future with hope

Guilt vs. remorse

Adversity	<ul><li>You have broken your moral code</li><li>You have failed to live up to your moral code</li><li>You have hurt someone's feelings</li></ul>	
Basic attitude	**RIGID AND EXTREME**	**FLEXIBLE AND NON-EXTREME**
Emotion	Guilt	Remorse
Behaviour	<ul><li>You escape from the unhealthy pain of guilt in self-defeating ways</li><li>You beg forgiveness from the person you have wronged</li><li>You promise unrealistically that you will not "sin" again</li><li>You punish yourself physically or by deprivation</li><li>You defensively disclaim responsibility for wrongdoing</li><li>You make excuses for your behaviour</li><li>You reject offers of forgiveness</li></ul>	<ul><li>You face up to the healthy pain that accompanies the realisation that you have "sinned"</li><li>You ask, but do not beg, for forgiveness</li><li>You understand the reasons for your wrongdoing and act on your understanding</li><li>You atone for the "sin" by taking a penalty</li><li>You make appropriate amends</li><li>You do not make excuses for your behaviour or enact other defensive behaviour</li><li>You accept offers for forgiveness</li></ul>
Subsequent thinking	<ul><li>You conclude that you have definitely committed the sin</li><li>You assume more personal responsibility than the situation warrants</li><li>You assign far less responsibility to others than is warranted</li><li>You dismiss possible mitigating factors for your behaviour</li><li>You only see your behaviour in a guilt-related context and fail to put it into an overall context</li><li>You think that you will receive retribution</li></ul>	<ul><li>You take into account all relevant data when judging whether or not you have "sinned"</li><li>You assume an appropriate level of personal responsibility</li><li>You assign an appropriate level of responsibility to others</li><li>You take into account mitigating factors</li><li>You put your behaviour into overall context</li><li>You think you may be penalised rather than receive retribution</li></ul>

Shame vs. disappointment

Adversity	• Something highly negative has been revealed about you (or about a group with whom you identify) by yourself or by others • You have acted in a way that falls very short of your ideal • Others look down on or shun you (or a group with whom you identify) or think that they do	
Basic attitude	**RIGID AND EXTREME**	**FLEXIBLE AND NON-EXTREME**
Emotion	**Shame**	**Disappointment**
Behaviour	• You remove yourself from the "gaze" of others • You isolate yourself from others • You save face by attacking other(s) who have "shamed" you • You defend your threatened self-esteem in self-defeating ways • You ignore attempts by others to restore social equilibrium	• You continue to participate actively in social interaction • You respond positively to attempts of others to restore social equilibrium
Subsequent thinking	• You overestimate the negativity of the information revealed • You overestimate the likelihood that the judging group will notice or be interested in the information • You overestimate the degree of disapproval you (or your reference group) will receive • You overestimate how long any disapproval will last	• You see the information revealed in a compassionate self-accepting context • You are realistic about the likelihood that the judging group will notice or be interested in the information revealed • You are realistic about the degree of disapproval self (or reference group) will receive • You are realistic about how long any disapproval will last

Hurt vs. sorrow

Adversity	• Others treat you badly (and you think you do not deserve such treatment) • You think that the other person has devalued your relationship (i.e. someone indicates that their relationship with you is less important to them than the relationship is to you)	
Basic attitude	**RIGID AND EXTREME**	**FLEXIBLE AND NON-EXTREME**
Emotion	Hurt	Sorrow
Behaviour	• You stop communicating with the other person	• You communicate your feelings to the other directly
Behaviour	• You sulk and make obvious you feel hurt without disclosing details of the matter • You indirectly criticise or punish the other person for their offence • You tell others how badly you have been treated, but don't take any responsibility for any contribution you may have made to this	• You request that the other person acts in a fairer manner towards you • You discuss the situation with others in a balanced way, focusing on the way you have been treated and taking responsibility for any contribution you may have made to this
Subsequent thinking	• You overestimate the unfairness of the other person's behaviour • You think that the other person does not care for you or is indifferent to you • You see yourself as alone, uncared for or misunderstood • You tend to think of past "hurts" • You think that the other person has to make the first move to you and you dismiss the possibility of making the first move towards that person	• You are realistic about the degree of unfairness in the other person's behaviour • You think that the other person has acted badly rather than demonstrated lack of caring or indifference • You see yourself as being in a poor situation, but still connected to, cared for by and understood by others not directly involved in the situation • If you think of past hurts you do so with less frequency and less intensity than when you feel hurt • You are open to the idea of making the first move towards the other person

Unhealthy anger vs. healthy anger

Adversity	• You think that you have been frustrated in some way or your movement towards an important goal has been obstructed in some way • Someone has treated you badly • Someone has transgressed one of your personal rules • You have transgressed one of your own personal rules • Someone or something has threatened your self-esteem or disrespected you	
Basic attitude	RIGID AND EXTREME	FLEXIBLE AND NON-EXTREME
Emotion	Unhealthy anger	Healthy anger
Behaviour	• You attack the other(s) physically	• You assert yourself with the other(s)
Behaviour	• You attack the other(s) verbally • You attack the other(s) passive-aggressively • You displace the attack on to another person, animal or object • You withdraw aggressively • You recruit allies against the other(s)	• You request, but do not demand, behavioural change from the other(s) • You leave an unsatisfactory situation non-aggressively after taking steps to deal with it
Subsequent thinking	• You overestimate the extent to which the other(s) acted deliberately • You see malicious intent in the motives of the other(s) • You see yourself as definitely right and the other(s) as definitely wrong • You are unable to see the point of view of the other(s) • You plot to exact revenge • You ruminate about the other's behaviour and imagine coming out on top	• You think that the other(s) may have acted deliberately, but you also recognise that this may not have been the case • You are able to see the point of view of the other(s) • You have fleeting, rather than sustained thoughts to exact revenge • You think that other(s) may have had malicious intent in their motives, but you also recognise that this may not have been the case • You think that you are probably rather than definitely right and the other(s) are probably rather than definitely wrong

Unhealthy jealousy vs. concern for your relationship (healthy jealousy)

Adversity	<ul><li>A threat is posed to your relationship with your partner from a third person</li><li>A threat is posed by the uncertainty you face concerning your partner's whereabouts, behaviour or thinking in the context of the first threat</li></ul>	
Basic attitude	**RIGID AND EXTREME**	**FLEXIBLE AND NON-EXTREME**
Emotion	**Unhealthy jealousy**	**Concern for your relationship (healthy jealousy)**
Behaviour	<ul><li>You monitor the actions and feelings of your partner</li></ul>	<ul><li>You allow your partner to initiate expressing love for you without prompting her or seeking reassurance once she has done so</li></ul>
Behaviour	<ul><li>You search for evidence that your partner is involved with someone else</li><li>You attempt to restrict the movements or activities of your partner</li><li>You set tests which your partner has to pass</li><li>You retaliate for your partner's presumed infidelity</li><li>You sulk</li></ul>	<ul><li>You allow your partner freedom without monitoring his/her feelings, actions and whereabouts</li><li>You allow your partner to show natural interest in members of the opposite sex without setting tests</li><li>You communicate your concern for your relationship in an open and non-blaming manner</li></ul>
Subsequent thinking	<ul><li>You exaggerate any threat to your relationship that does exist</li><li>You think the loss of your relationship is imminent</li><li>You misconstrue your partner's ordinary conversations with relevant others as having romantic or sexual connotations</li><li>You construct visual images of your partner's infidelity</li><li>If your partner admits to finding another person attractive, you think that s/he finds that person more attractive than you and that s/he will leave you for this other person</li></ul>	<ul><li>You tend not to exaggerate any threat to your relationship that does exist</li><li>You do not misconstrue ordinary conversations between your partner and another man/woman</li><li>You do not construct visual images of your partner's infidelity</li><li>You accept that your partner will find others attractive but you do not see this as a threat</li></ul>

Unhealthy envy vs. healthy envy

Adversity	• Another person possesses and enjoys something desirable that you do not have	
Basic attitude	**RIGID AND EXTREME**	**FLEXIBLE AND NON-EXTREME**
Emotion	**Unhealthy envy**	**Healthy envy**
Behaviour	• You disparage verbally to others the person who has the desired possession • You disparage verbally to others the desired possession	• You strive to obtain the desired possession if it is truly what you want
Behaviour	• If you had the chance you would take away the desired possession from the other (either so that you will have it or that the other is deprived of it) • If you had the chance you would spoil or destroy the desired possession so that the other person does not have it	
Subsequent thinking	• You tend to denigrate in your mind the value of the desired possession and/or the person who possesses it You try to convince yourself that you are happy with your possessions (although you are not) • You think about how to acquire the desired possession regardless of its usefulness • You think about how to deprive the other person of the desired possession • You think about how to spoil or destroy the other's desired possession • You think about all the other things the other has that you don't have	• You honestly admit to yourself that you desire the desired possession You are honest with yourself if you are not happy with your possessions, rather than defensively try to convince yourself that you are happy with them when you are not • You think about how to obtain the desired possession because you desire it for healthy reasons • You can allow the other person to have and enjoy the desired possession without denigrating that person or possession • You think about what the other has and lacks and what you have and lack

Appendix 2

Corrie Inspiration Inventory

The Inspiration Inventory

The purpose of the Inspiration Inventory[1] is to help you review the core domains of your life so that you can become clearer about what's working really well, which areas need a little refining and which need some major attention.

Take your time to think about the core domains listed in the table below and then rate each one from 0 to 10 according to how satisfied and fulfilled you feel (where 0 = a total lack of satisfaction and fulfilment; 10 = totally fulfilled and satisfied).

The Inspiration Inventory

1	**Overall happiness and emotional well-being:** Prompt Questions: Do you enjoy your life? Are you glad just to be alive? Does your life inspire you or are you often anxious, disillusioned or unhappy?	0 1 2 3 4 5 6 7 8 9 10
2	**Relationship to self:** Prompt Questions: Do you respect the person that you are? Are you at peace with yourself, confident in your abilities or do you worry about coming up to scratch?	0 1 2 3 4 5 6 7 8 9 10
3	**Intimate relationships:** Prompt Questions: Do you feel loved, appreciated and supported by those that matter to you? Can you express emotional and physical intimacy easily? Can you give and receive love freely?	0 1 2 3 4 5 6 7 8 9 10

The Inspiration Inventory

4	**Friendships and social life:** Prompt Questions: Do you have good friendships based on mutual respect and trust? Can you be yourself in your friendships or do you feel pressurised to be someone you are not?	0 1 2 3 4 5 6 7 8 9 10
5	**Health:** Prompt Questions: Do you have abundant energy? Do you respect and nurture your body? Do you nourish yourself with healthy foods, sufficient sleep and time to relax and unwind?	0 1 2 3 4 5 6 7 8 9 10
6	**Lifestyle and work–life balance:** Prompt Questions: Does your lifestyle reflect and honour your priorities? Do you have a good work–life balance or often feel exhausted or "burnt out"?	0 1 2 3 4 5 6 7 8 9 10
7	**Career and work:** Prompt Questions: Do you enjoy your work? Does it inspire you and enrich your life? Does it allow you to express your talents and abilities? Does your work sustain or undermine you?	0 1 2 3 4 5 6 7 8 9 10
8	**Money and finances:** Prompt Questions: Do you have sufficient money to meet your needs? Are you satisfied with your income? Do you have a system for organising your finances, including outgoings, savings and pension?	0 1 2 3 4 5 6 7 8 9 10
9	**Hobbies and leisure interests:** Prompt Questions: Do you have fulfilling hobbies and interests separate from your work? Do you have sufficient time for this part of your life or is it often eroded by work or other pressures?	0 1 2 3 4 5 6 7 8 9 10
10	**Values and principles:** Prompt Questions: Are you clear what you stand for? Are you living life according to your core values? Are there any areas of your life in which you compromise your values?	0 1 2 3 4 5 6 7 8 9 10
11	**Community and contribution:** Do you feel you make a difference to the world, even in a small way? Do others benefit from your talents and gifts?	0 1 2 3 4 5 6 7 8 9 10

The Inspiration Inventory

12	**Spiritual life:** Prompt Questions: Is there space in your life to develop your potential, your expanded self and your spiritual self? Do you feel the need to belong to a religious or spiritual community? If so, is this need being met?	0 1 2 3 4 5 6 7 8 9 10
13	**Any other area important to you** **Name it here:** .... Prompt Questions: What other areas of your life really matter to you and which are not included in the above?	0 1 2 3 4 5 6 7 8 9 10

> Helpful hint: You can select as many areas as you like, but depending on how many core themes you think need attention, you may find it helpful to select just one or two to begin with.

Helpful hint: As you go through the Inspiration Inventory, think about where you are now in each of these areas compared with five years ago. Are the results favourable or not? This will help you interpret your scores in the light of your recent life history.

Interpreting your results

Any areas where you scored between 8 and 10 are core domains which are working very well for you and from which you are drawing a sense of fulfilment and inspiration. Check back over your responses. In how many areas of your life did you score 8–10?

- 8–10 = a core domain in which you are fulfilled and which probably does not need attention right now. I scored ... of these

Any areas where you scored between 4 and 7 are areas that may need some attention, although they may not be your immediate priority. Check back over your responses. In how many areas of your life did you score 4–7?

- 4–7 = a core domain that needs some attention at some point. I scored ... of these

Any areas where you scored between 0–3 require some urgent attention and so you will probably want to prioritise these. Check back over your responses. In how many areas of your life did you score 0–3?

- 0–3 = a core domain that needs immediate attention. I scored … of these

So how did you do? In which areas did you score the highest? Which were the areas in which you scored the lowest? What do your scores tell you about the quality of your life and what needs to change?

What's working well?

Let's start by looking at those areas of your life that are going well – those areas where you gave yourself a rating of 8 or more. These areas give you a clue about the strengths, talents and resources you already have available to you – the same strengths and resources you will need to bring to those areas you are wanting to change. So think about the role you have played in creating these results. What skills, talents, attitudes and outlooks have helped you create these effects for yourself? Record your thoughts in the space below.

The reason my life is working well in these areas is because:
_____
_____
_____
_____

What might need some attention (at some stage)?

Now look at those areas where you scored between 4 and 7. You are experiencing some degree of satisfaction, but not as much as you would like. Chances are you feel that these areas of your life will need attention at some point in the future. See if you can identify what's getting in the way here. What attitudes or beliefs are holding you back? Which of your skills and talents are not being used to their full potential? How are you currently organising your life that prevents you from giving yourself a rating from 8 to 10? Write your thoughts in the space below.

The reason why these areas of my life are not working as well as I would like are:
_____
_____
_____
_____

What definitely needs to change?

Now let's look at those areas where you are dissatisfied, unfulfilled or seriously uninspired (any area where you gave yourself a score between 0 and 3). Just like your strengths, the core areas you have identified contain some important clues about you, your values and how you have chosen to organise your life. So see if you can work out why you have struggled in these areas. It may be that you are currently missing some important skills or knowledge, or that old habits of thinking, feeling and behaving are undermining your attempts to succeed. Make a note of anything that seems relevant in the space below.

The reason I am struggling in these areas is because:

_____
_____
_____
_____

Selecting your core domains for self-coaching

Once you have a clearer picture of the core areas that are working well and those that aren't, you are in a stronger position to coach yourself to success. Based on the results of your Inspiration Inventory, what do you think are the most important domains to work on right now?

_____
_____
_____
_____

Once you have identified the core domains for your coaching journey, double check them against the following questions:

- Six months from now, what would you *most* like to be different?
- What would you like more of in your life?
- What, if anything, would you like less of?
- How will you know when you've achieved the results you are looking for?
  - How will you feel?
  - How will you think about yourself, others and life in general?
  - How will you organise your life differently?

Now pull it all together. If you review all your answers, what is the area (or areas) you are going to focus on right now?

The core area/s in which I most want to coach myself is/are:
_____
_____
_____
_____

If you have worked through the previous exercises, you will now have a clear idea of the key area or areas that are going to be the focus of your self-coaching.

Note

1 This was originally published in *The Art of Inspired Living: Coach Yourself with Positive Psychology*, by Sarah Corrie (Karnac Books, 2009), and is reprinted with kind permission of Karnac Books and Sarah Corrie.

References

Bannister, D., & Fransella, F. (1986). *Inquiring man: The psychology of personal constructs.* London: Croom-Helm.

Bordin, E.S. (1979). The generalizability of the psychoanalytic concept of the working alliance. *Psychotherapy: Theory, Research and Practice,* 16, 252–60.

Blonna, R. (2010). *Maximize your coaching effectiveness with acceptance and commitment therapy.* Oakland, CA: New Harbinger Publications.

Brickhill, P. (1954). *Reach for the sky: The story of Douglas Bader DSO, DFC.* London: Collins.

Carter, A. (2006). *Practical methods for evaluating coaching.* Brighton, East Sussex: Institute for Employment Studies.

Cavanagh, M.J. (2005). Mental-health issues and challenging clients in executive coaching. In M.J. Cavanagh, A.M. Grant & T. Kemp (Eds), *Evidence-based coaching: Theory, research and practice from the behavioural sciences* (pp. 21–36). Bowen Hills QLD: Australian Academic Press.

Cooper, M., & Dryden, W. (2016). Introduction to pluralistic counselling and psychotherapy. In M. Cooper & W. Dryden (Eds), *The handbook of pluralistic counselling and psychotherapy* (pp. 1–11). London: Sage.

Dorn, F.J. (Ed.). (1984). *The social influence process in counseling and psychotherapy.* Springfield, IL: Charles C. Thomas.

Dryden, W. (1985). Challenging but not overwhelming: A compromise in negotiating homework assignments. *British Journal of Cognitive Psychotherapy,* 3(1), 77–80.

Dryden, W. (2006). *Counselling in a nutshell.* London: Sage.

Dryden, W. (2011). *Counselling in a nutshell. 2nd edition.* London: Sage.

Dryden, W. (2017). *Very brief cognitive-behavioural coaching.* Abingdon, Oxon: Routledge.

Garvin, C.D., & Seabury, B.A. (1997). *Interpersonal practice in social work: Promoting competence and social justice. 2nd edition.* Boston, MA: Allyn & Bacon.

Gessnitzer, S., & Kauffeld, S. (2015). The working alliance in coaching: Why behaviour is the key to success. *The Journal of Applied Behavioral Science,* 51, 177–97.

Grant, A.M., & Cavanagh, M.J. (2010). Life coaching. In E. Cox, T. Bachkirova & D. Clutterbuck (Eds), *The complete handbook of coaching* (pp. 297–310). London: Sage.

Gray, D.E. (2004). Principles and processes in coaching evaluation. *International Journal of Mentoring and Coaching,* 2(2). Online at: www.emccouncil.org/uk/journal.htm.

Gyllensten, K., & Palmer, S. (2007). The coaching relationship: An interpretative phenomenological analysis. *International Coaching Psychology Review*, 2(2), 168–76.

Hutchins, D.E. (1984). Improving the counseling relationship. *Personnel and Guidance Journal*, 62, 572–5.

Iordanou, I., Hawley, R., & Iordanou, C. (2017). *Values and ethics in coaching.* London: Sage Publications.

Iveson, C., George, E., & Ratner, H. (2012). *Brief coaching: A solution-focused approach.* Hove, East Sussex: Routledge.

Jiang, J. (2016). *Rejection proof: How to beat fear and become invincible.* London: Random House Books.

Joseph, S. (2013). *What doesn't kill us: A guide to overcoming adversity and moving forward.* London: Piatkus.

Korotitsch, W.J., & Nelson-Gray, R.O. (1999). An overview of self-monitoring research in assessment and treatment. *Psychological Assessment*, 11, 415–25.

Lazarus, A.A. (1989). *The practice of multi-modal therapy: Systematic, comprehensive and effective psychotherapy.* Baltimore, MD: The Johns Hopkins University Press.

Lazarus, A.A. (1993). Tailoring the therapeutic relationship, or being an authentic chameleon. *Psychotherapy: Theory, Research & Practice*, 30, 404–7.

Neenan, M. (2017). *Developing resilience: A cognitive-behavioural approach.* 2nd Edition. Abingdon, Oxon: Routledge.

Nezu, A.M., Maguth Nezu, C., & D'Zurilla, T.J. (2013). *Problem-solving therapy: A treatment manual.* New York: Springer Publishing Co.

O'Broin, A., & Palmer, S. (2006). The coach–client relationship and contributions made by the coach in improving coaching outcome. *The Coaching Psychologist*, 2(2), 16–20.

O'Broin, A., & Palmer, S. (2010a). The coaching alliance as a universal concept spanning conceptual approaches. *Coaching Psychology International*, 3(1), 3–6.

O'Broin, A., & Palmer, S. (2010b). Exploring key aspects in the formation of coaching relationships: Initial indicators from the perspective of the coachee and the coach. *Coaching: An International Journal of Theory, Research and Practice*, 3, 124–43.

Palmer, S. (2008). The PRACTICE model of coaching: Towards a solution-focused approach. *Coaching Psychology International*, 1(1), 4–6.

Pinsof, W.M., & Catherall, D. (1986). The integrative psychotherapy alliance: Family, couple, individual therapy scales. *Journal of Marital and Family Therapy*, 12, 137–51.

Rescher, N. (1993). *Pluralism: Against the demand for consensus.* Oxford: Oxford University Press.

Rogers, C.R. (1957). The necessary and sufficient conditions of therapeutic personality change. *Journal of Consulting Psychology*, 21, 95–103.

Whitten, H. (2009). *Cognitive behavioural coaching techniques for dummies.* Chichester, West Sussex: John Wiley & Sons.

Index

ABC framework 19
Acceptance and Commitment Coaching 19
action tendencies 20, 84–5, 91
adversities 82, 83, 84–5, 95, 145–6, 147, 151–9
applicants 31, 46
assessment process 46, 47–50, 120–2; Edward 99–100; Kirsten 129–31; Lionel 64–6
assignment tasks 95–6

basic attitudes 12, 16–19, 82, 83, 86, 93–4, 95, 111–13; EPF-CEBC 86, 87, 88, 89, 93–4, 96–7, 104–6
Beck, A.T. 81
behaviour 11, 20–1, 84–5, 151–9
bonds 27–30
Bordin, E.S. 27, 120
brainstorming 58

calculated risk *see* risk-taking
Cavanagh, M.J. 31, 51, 80
CBC (cognitive-behavioural coaching) 2, 18, 23, 34
CEBC (cognitive-emotive-behavioural coaching) 1, 2–3, 10–11, 36–7, 38–44, 46, 60–2
clients 29, 41, 46
coachee role 31, 46, 47
coaches 1, 2, 22–3, 25, 30, 52, 142–3, 149
coaching 1–2, 22–3, 25, 31–6, 61, 142–3, 149
coaching alliance 27, 35, 93, 120; bonds 27–30; goals 36, 37–8; negotiated consent 3, 7, 30–1, 36, 40, 47, 50, 52; tasks 27, 38–44, 94–5; views 27, 30–6

coaching approaches 1, 6, 7, 22–3, 24–5, 36, 40
coaching relationship 2, 3, 4, 6–7, 8
cognition 11–18, 21
cognitive-behavioural coaching *see* CBC
cognitive-emotive-behavioural coaching *see* CEBC
confidentiality 35
contracts 30, 50–4, 121, 149; Edward 100; Kirsten 130; Lionel 65, 66–9, 98
core attitudes 17–18
core conditions 27, 28
Corrie Inspiration Inventory 123, 160–5

DF-CEBC (development-focused cognitive-emotive-behavioural coaching) 2, 3, 4, 31, 33, 49, 110–18, 119–20, 125–7; assessment process 120–2; behaviour 20–1; coaching relationship 3, 4, 6–7; contracts 52, 53; emotions 19; inferential distortions 12; objectives 3, 4, 6, 36–7, 114–15, 122–5, 132–3, 135–9; process 3, 4, 6; *see also* Kirsten
dialectical engagement 86, 93, 104–6
discomfort tolerance 115, 132
distortions 12, 13–16, 96–7
Dryden, W. 2, 27, 30, 48, 95, 121, 122; *see also* Kirsten

eclecticism (integration) 23
Edward (EPF-CEBC example) 97, 98, 99; assessment process 99–100; contract 100; dialectical engagement 105–6; initial contact 99; Situational ABCDEFG framework 100–4, 105–8
Ellis, A. 81, 110